BASIC MATH

AGS

by
Donald H. Jacobs, M.Ed.
and
August V. Treff, M.Ed.

AGS®

American Guidance Service, Inc.
4201 Woodland Road
Circle Pines, MN 55014-1796
1-800-328-2560

Printed in the United States of America

ISBN 0–7854–0955–6 (Previously ISBN 0–88671–970–4)

Product Number 90863

A 0 9 8 7 6 5 4 5 3

Contents

Comparing Numbers

Use the = sign to show that one number is *equal* to another number.

2 = 2   38 = 38   719 = 719

Use the < sign to show that one number is *less* than another number.

When we read this, 6 < 11, we say, "Six is less than eleven."

Use the > sign to show that one number is *greater* than another number.

When we read this, 8 > 3, we say, "Eight is greater than three."

The signs < and > will always point to the smaller number.

Write the correct symbol for each pair of numbers. Use the =, <, or > sign.

1. 8 ◯ 2   2. 13 ◯ 20   3. 28 ◯ 16

4. 23 ◯ 20   5. 10 ◯ 29   6. 12 ◯ 23

7. 34 ◯ 34   8. 4 ◯ 10   9. 34 ◯ 32

10. 11 ◯ 12   11. 10 ◯ 23   12. 10 ◯ 54

13. 56 ◯ 53   14. 101 ◯ 210   15. 0 ◯ 1

16. 18 ◯ 16   17. 39 ◯ 23   18. 6 ◯ 6

19. 0 ◯ 50   20. 58 ◯ 58   21. 15 ◯ 10

22. 1 ◯ 0   23. 8 ◯ 15   24. 104 ◯ 103

 The Blue Streak played the Comets for the city basketball championship. The Blue Streak scored 74 points; the Comets scored 59 points. Which team scored more points?

_____

In one year, there were 5,980,981 cars produced in the United States.

This chart shows the place values of all the digits in the number 5,980,981.

Example: What is the place value of each underlined digit?
5,980,981 **millions**
5,980,981 **thousands**

Millions	Hundred-thousands	Ten-thousands	Thousands	Hundreds	Tens	Ones
5	9	8	0	9	8	1

Write the place value for each of the underlined digits.

1. 2,963 _____
2. 4,966 _____
3. 96,000 _____
4. 70,005 _____
5. 107,022 _____
6. 23,441 _____
7. 10,234 _____
8. 30,232 _____
9. 257,231 _____
10. 85,401 _____
11. 3,023 _____
12. 211 _____
13. 302,021 _____
14. 4,394,100 _____
15. 12,345,567 _____
16. 92,332,110 _____
17. 45,234 _____
18. 203,240 _____
19. 10,612 _____
20. 653,864 _____
21. 9,038 _____
22. 67,824 _____
23. 298,344 _____
24. 733,200 _____
25. 72,131 _____
26. 344,512 _____
27. 29,290 _____
28. 53,102 _____
29. 94 _____
30. 1,111,111 _____

Numbers in Expanded Form

U N I T 1

The City Library received new books in six shipments:

a. 700,000   **b.** 90,000   **c.** 8,000   **d.** 600   **e.** 10   **f.** 8

How many books did the library receive?

700,000	The 7 means 7 hundred-thousands
90,000	The 9 means 9 ten-thousands
8,000	The 8 means 8 thousands
600	The 6 means 6 hundreds
10	The 1 means 1 ten
+ 8	The 8 means 8 ones
798,618	Total number of books the library received

700,000 + 90,000 + 8,000 + 600 + 10 + 8   798,618
     This is the **expanded** form.   This is the **standard** form.

 Write the standard form for each of these numbers. They are written below in expanded form.

1. 5,000 + 600 + 80 + 4 = _____

2. 8,000 + 700 + 30 = _____

3. 90,000 + 200 + 70 = _____

4. 50,000 + 200 + 70 = _____

5. 90,000 + 3,000 + 600 + 10 + 3 = _____

6. 400,000 + 20,000 + 9,000 + 600 + 40 + 7 = _____

7. 100,000 + 90,000 + 3,000 + 200 + 80 + 1 = _____

8. 700,000 + 20,000 + 5,000 + 400 + 30 + 9 = _____

9. 2,000 + 600 + 90 = _____

10. 30,000 + 3,000 + 500 + 60 + 2 = _____

11. 10,000 + 4,000 + 70 + 4 = _____

12. 20,000 + 600 + 90 = _____

13. 8,000 + 700 + 10 + 5 = _____

14. 500,000 + 70,000 + 3,000 + 800 + 40 + 9 = _____

15. 60,000 + 3,000 + 200 + 80 + 6 = _____

16. 200,000 + 90,000 + 2,000 + 400 + 7 = _____

 Use the + key on a calculator to see the number of miles Miguel Indurain of Spain pedaled. He pedaled 2,000 + 400 + 70 + 4 miles to win the Tour de France bicycle race.

Miguel Indurain rode _____ miles

Writing Numbers in Expanded Form

The land area of the United States is 3,536,278 square miles.
Write the number of square miles in expanded form.

3,536,278 = 3,000,000 + 500,000 + 30,000 + 6,000 + 200 + 70 + 8

 Write these numbers in expanded form.

1. 276 = _____

2. 4,185 = _____

3. 5,023 = _____

4. 16,383 = _____

5. 24,076 = _____

6. 49,208 = _____

7. 18,234 = _____

8. 213,537 = _____

9. 4,687,654 = _____

10. 123,218 = _____

11. 42,721 = _____

12. 5,817,295 = _____

13. 7,182,998 = _____

14. 54,281 = _____

15. 1,445,123 = _____

16. 570,821 = _____

17. 2,857 = _____

18. 72,695 = _____

19. 389,426 = _____

20. 9,999,999 = _____

Translating Number Words

During a round-the-world flight, a jet traveled twenty-six thousand, three hundred eighty-two miles.

If we write the distance in standard form, we find that

Twenty-six thousand, three hundred eighty-two = 26,382

Write these number words in standard form.

1. four hundred thirty-five = _____

2. fifty-seven = _____

3. nine hundred eighty-nine = _____

4. thirty-three thousand = _____

5. six thousand, five = _____

6. two thousand, seventy-nine = _____

7. seven thousand, eight hundred forty-five = _____

8. nine thousand, four hundred thirteen = _____

9. six hundred two thousand, eleven = _____

10. seventy-three thousand, one hundred twenty-four _____

11. forty-six thousand, nine hundred eighty-seven _____

12. five hundred eleven thousand, three hundred _____

13. two hundred six thousand, nine hundred seventy-eight = _____

14. forty-four thousand, two hundred fifty-five = _____

15. eleven thousand, six hundred one = _____

16. three hundred forty-nine thousand, three = _____

17. seventy-two thousand, one hundred sixty-five = _____

18. eight hundred thirty-six thousand, seven hundred twenty-three = _____

19. two hundred eighty-nine thousand, sixty-four = _____

20. one hundred thousand, nine hundred = _____

 Mt. McKinley is twenty thousand, three hundred twenty feet high. Circle the height of Mt. McKinley written in standard number form.

   a. 2,032 feet   **b.** 2,320 feet   **c.** 20,320 feet   **d.** 23,020 feet

UNIT 1

In one year, there were 414,375 flights from San Francisco International Airport. If we write the number of flights in words, this is what it would look like

    four hundred fourteen thousand, three hundred seventy-five

Handy Reference for Spelling				
one	seven	thirteen	nineteen	sixty-five
two	eight	fourteen	twenty	seventy-six
three	nine	fifteen	twenty-one	eighty-seven
four	ten	sixteen	thirty-two	ninety-eight
five	eleven	seventeen	forty-three	hundred
six	twelve	eighteen	fifty-four	thousand

■ Write these numbers in words.

1. 168 = _____

2. 262 = _____

3. 506 = _____

4. 720 = _____

5. 1,246 = _____

6. 3,405 = _____

7. 19,117 = _____

8. 23,340 = _____

9. 45,103 = _____

10. 43,978 = _____

11. 90,003 = _____

12. 160,519 = _____

13. 704,230 = _____

14. 569,102 = _____

15. 18,473 = _____

16. 245,246 = _____

17. 83,900 = _____

18. 967,511 = _____

19. 13,994 = _____

20. 880,312 = _____

Rounding Numbers

When you round numbers, follow these steps.

Example:
Round 2,831 to the nearest hundred.
Step 1: Find the place value.   2,831
Step 2: Check digit to the immediate right of that place.   2,831
Step 3: If the digit is less than 5, replace it, and any other digits to the right, with zeros.   **2,800**

Example:
Round 5,874 to the nearest thousand.
Step 1: Find the place value.   5,874
Step 2: Check digit to the immediate right of that place.   5,874
Step 3: If the digit is more than 5, add 1 to the place value number. Replace the digits to the right with zeros.   **6,000**

Zeros always replace digits to the right of the rounded place value.

 Round these numbers to the indicated place.

Tens	Hundreds	Thousands
1. 62 _____	13. 38,234 _____	25. 4,129 _____
2. 3,629 _____	14. 7,185 _____	26. 9,562 _____
3. 7 _____	15. 738 _____	27. 8,299 _____
4. 3,900 _____	16. 3,209 _____	28. 4,623 _____
5. 54,212 _____	17. 48 _____	29. 15,500 _____
6. 34,089 _____	18. 3,293 _____	30. 7,967 _____
7. 5,219 _____	19. 6,432 _____	31. 29,345 _____
8. 317 _____	20. 8,325 _____	32. 203,122 _____
9. 18 _____	21. 762 _____	33. 2,900 _____
10. 685 _____	22. 321 _____	34. 34,550 _____
11. 43 _____	23. 14,209 _____	35. 599 _____
12. 512 _____	24. 1,692 _____	36. 500 _____

 The residents of Columbia City released 54,689 red, white, and blue balloons to celebrate Independence Day. How many balloons, to the nearest thousandth, were released?

_____

Adding Whole Numbers

The order in which you add two numbers does not change the sum.

Example: Add 8 and 5.

8	Addend	OR	5	Addend
+ 5	Addend		+ 8	Addend
13	Sum		13	Sum

Adding zero to a number does not change the number.

Example: Add 4 and 0.

    4   OR   0
 + 0   + 4
   4   4

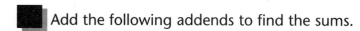 Add the following addends to find the sums.

1.
0	1	3	5	7	9	2	5	5	7	3	2	3	5	1
+1	+1	+4	+9	+8	+5	+0	+6	+3	+3	+1	+7	+7	+5	+4

2.
9	9	8	8	7	6	4	5	2	2	8	4	5	3	7
+2	+4	+3	+4	+4	+3	+5	+7	+5	+9	+5	+4	+0	+4	+4

3.
6	2	2	9	8	7	8	4	7	3	5	9	0	8	4
+8	+7	+6	+0	+5	+7	+2	+9	+6	+5	+5	+6	+4	+1	+2

4.
4	3	6	9	8	3	7	4	4	5	5	9	4	8	3
+6	+3	+5	+7	+8	+2	+0	+4	+0	+5	+2	+8	+7	+3	+0

5.
5	4	7	8	9	0	3	6	8	6	4	7	1	5	1
+0	+3	+9	+6	+1	+8	+0	+1	+1	+7	+5	+8	+5	+9	+0

Addition

When you are adding two-digit numbers,
add the ones first. Then add the tens.

Example:

```
   37          3|7
  + 2         +|2
   39          3|9
```

tens / ones

Sometimes the sum of two numbers in a column is more than 9.

Example: 48 + 5 = 53
Add the ones first. 8 + 5 = 13
Write the 3 in the ones column.
Write the 1, which represents 10, in the tens column.
Add the tens. 1 + 4 = 5.

```
    ¹
   48
  + 5
    3
```

```
    ¹
   48
  + 5
   53
```

Add the following addends.

1.
24	16	35	14	21	54	68	33
+ 5	+ 3	+ 2	+ 3	+ 8	+ 7	+ 6	+ 9

2.
58	63	90	49	25	68	57	23
+ 32	+ 45	+ 63	+ 66	+ 61	+ 56	+ 94	+ 35

3.
305	103	275	333	301	995	47	73
+ 621	+ 611	+ 600	+ 895	+ 563	+ 678	+ 45	+ 88

4.
2	4	3	6	3	6	9	1
4	5	1	9	2	8	3	7
+ 5	+ 2	+ 2	+ 4	+ 7	+ 3	+ 7	+ 9

5.
28	93	50	97	62	25	73	92
54	23	10	85	34	35	38	69
+ 90	+ 74	+ 83	+ 34	+ 18	+ 66	+ 75	+ 34

6.
278	105	895	461	700	205	196	673
495	932	812	158	621	511	262	115
+ 339	+ 409	+ 527	+ 405	+ 299	+ 388	+ 428	+ 137

 Use the + key on a calculator to find the sum. Two years ago, 141 students participated in the school sports program. Last year, 186 participated. This year, 296 students enrolled in the program. How many students participated in the school sports program during the past three years?

_____

Subtracting Whole Numbers

When we subtract whole numbers, we line up the numbers in the correct columns.

Example: Subtract: 28 – 5

28	**Minuend**
– 5	**Subtrahend**
23	**Difference**

Example: Subtract: 9 – 6   Subtract: 57 – 21

```
    9                         57
  – 6                       – 21
    3                         36
```

 Subtract to find the differences. Add to check your answers.

1. 9
    – 4

2. 8
    – 3

3. 7
    – 6

4. 9
    – 5

5. 5
    – 4

6. 8
    – 5

7. 7
    – 7

8. 8
    – 0

9. 9
    – 2

10. 6
     – 5

11. 12
     – 2

12. 25
     – 14

13. 42
     – 31

14. 18
     – 8

15. 27
     – 27

16. 298
     – 35

17. 394
     – 52

18. 158
     – 26

19. 166
     – 46

20. 453
     – 20

21. 698
     – 223

22. 734
     – 202

23. 282
     – 100

24. 956
     – 235

25. 755
     – 120

26. 4,576
     – 342

27. 4,594
     – 373

28. 3,857
     – 1,546

29. 6,206
     – 2,205

30. 4,865
     – 4,264

31. 6,598
     – 1,276

32. 7,547
     – 6,313

33. 6,289
     – 2,021

34. 4,836
     – 3,711

35. 9,385
     – 4,031

Subtraction with Renaming

Sometimes you must rename tens and ones in order to subtract.

Example: Subtract: 42 – 8

$$\begin{array}{r} {}^{3}\ ^{12} \\ \cancel{4}\cancel{2} \\ -\ 8 \\ \hline 34 \end{array}$$ because 12 – 8 = 4

More examples:

Subtract: 63 – 18

$$\begin{array}{r} {}^{5}\ ^{13} \\ \cancel{6}\cancel{3} \\ -\ 18 \\ \hline 45 \end{array}$$

Subtract: 358 – 89

$$\begin{array}{r} {}^{2}\ ^{14}\ ^{18} \\ \cancel{3}\cancel{5}\cancel{8} \\ -\ 89 \\ \hline 269 \end{array}$$

Subtract: 207 – 39

$$\begin{array}{r} {}^{19}\ ^{17} \\ \cancel{2}\cancel{0}\cancel{7} \\ -\ 39 \\ \hline 168 \end{array}$$

 Subtract. Rename as needed. Add to check your answers.

1. 26 – 7	2. 33 – 4	3. 72 – 8	4. 27 – 9	5. 88 – 9
6. 17 – 5	7. 41 – 22	8. 148 – 39	9. 565 – 17	10. 712 – 23
11. 834 – 25	12. 572 – 57	13. 733 – 34	14. 251 – 52	15. 521 – 124
16. 234 – 143	17. 304 – 215	18. 550 – 169	19. 812 – 675	20. 300 – 108
21. 2,833 – 345	22. 5,867 – 488	23. 7,503 – 225	24. 7,004 – 504	25. 1,004 – 455
26. 4,905 – 2,456	27. 8,033 – 1,734	28. 4,055 – 3,946	29. 2,003 – 1,205	30. 9,302 – 5,667

 Last June, 420 people applied for camping permits.
This June, 42 fewer people applied for permits.
How many people applied for permits this year?

_____

Subtraction Practice

 Subtract. Rename as needed. Add to check your answers.

1.

37	40	54	46	55	74	90
− 28	− 39	− 36	− 27	− 38	− 36	− 63

2.

75	82	80	21	48	35	67
− 66	− 54	− 52	− 18	− 39	− 17	− 19

3.

54	86	92	418	72	2,930	102
− 25	− 19	− 40	− 267	− 36	− 890	− 98

4.

763	7,098	867	1,763	35	203	510
− 475	− 6,419	− 154	− 423	− 29	− 66	− 71

5.

1,267	526	633	739	3,009	911	2,291
− 815	− 498	− 592	− 265	− 2,020	− 79	− 1,074

6.

209	1,029	258	55	12,837	4,009	6,123
− 78	− 490	− 146	− 29	− 2,933	− 836	− 662

7.

991	6,540	4,051	2,112	495	888	4,682
− 61	− 2,631	− 3,002	− 838	− 102	− 99	− 1,000

8.

4,820	9,163	5,032	9,100	4,103	8,300	9,651
− 785	− 562	− 863	− 1,629	−1,263	− 3,207	− 8,762

9.

9,283	8,763	6,938	9,137	8,163	8,752	7,900
− 2,691	− 874	− 3,848	− 2,281	− 5,545	− 3,964	− 6,802

10.

1,590	2,961	2,906	2,094	9,476	3,307	5,031
− 1,238	− 1,724	− 1,446	− 1,794	− 3,042	− 2,937	− 2,608

Estimating Sums and Differences

When you estimate, you use rounded numbers to do the computation.

Example: Estimate the sum of 394 + 214.
Step 1: Round 394 to 400.
Step 2: Round 214 to 200.
Step 3: Add the rounded numbers.
400 + 200 = 600

Example: Estimate the difference between 1,240 and 330.
Step 1: Round 1,240 to 1,200.
Step 2: Round 330 to 300.
Step 3: Subtract 300 from 1,200.
1,200 – 300 = 900

A Round to the nearest ten or hundred. Estimate.

1. 17 + 29 _____
2. 410 + 523 _____
3. 39 + 201 _____
4. 111 + 11 _____

5. 67 + 75 _____
6. 4 + 196 _____
7. 500 + 81 _____
8. 13 + 313 _____

9. 886 – 43 _____
10. 67 – 27 _____
11. 596 – 294 _____
12. 98 – 37 _____

13. 21 – 11 _____
14. 749 – 168 _____
15. 110 – 52 _____
16. 214 – 112 _____

B Estimate the sums and differences.

17. Kevin spent $14 at the music store, $49 at the shoe store, and $8 at the bookstore. How much did Kevin spend at the mall? _____

18. The Conways took a trip around the United States. The first week they drove 846 miles; the second week 1,211 miles; the third week 916 miles; and the fourth week 1,333 miles. How many miles did the Conways travel? Estimate to the nearest thousand. _____

19. Roberto was born in 1926. Sam was born in 1972. How much older is Roberto than Sam? _____

20. In March, 12,369 attended the symphony. A record-breaking crowd of 15,666 attended in May. How many more people went to the symphony in May? _____

Estimate your answer. Then use a calculator to check your estimate.

The three tallest buildings in Chicago are the Sears Tower at 1,454 feet; the Amoco Building at 1,136 feet, and the John Hancock Center at 1,127 feet. What is the combined height of these buildings?

_____

Beginning Multiplication

Addition and multiplication are related. Multiplication is a quick way to add the same number many times.

Addition:

```
   5      The addend 5 is
   5      used 3 times.
 + 5
 ────
  15
```

Multiplication: 3 x 5 = 15   OR

```
   5   Factor
 x 3   Factor
 ────
  15   Product
```

Examples: 3 x 8 = 24

```
    9
  x 6
  ───
   54
```

Example: Find the product of 38 and 2.

Step 1:
```
   ¹
   38   because
  x 2   2 x 8 = 16
  ───
    6
```

Step 2:
```
   ¹
   38   because
  x 2   2 x 3 = 6 and
  ───
   76   6 + 1 = 7
```

■ Multiply. Check your answers.

1. 4 x 3	2. 6 x 7	3. 5 x 6	4. 8 x 8	5. 6 x 4	6. 7 x 8	7. 9 x 7
8. 8 x 6	9. 2 x 7	10. 4 x 5	11. 6 x 0	12. 9 x 9	13. 5 x 5	14. 3 x 9
15. 6 x 6	16. 4 x 8	17. 3 x 5	18. 9 x 5	19. 7 x 2	20. 4 x 8	21. 3 x 8
22. 15 x 3	23. 34 x 6	24. 72 x 7	25. 19 x 4	26. 45 x 7	27. 66 x 5
28. 37 x 4	29. 22 x 7	30. 63 x 8	31. 89 x 3	32. 47 x 9	33. 51 x 6
34. 58 x 3	35. 72 x 8	36. 91 x 5	37. 24 x 4	38. 13 x9	39. 37 x 3
40. 82 x 3	41. 25 x 8	42. 39 x 5	43. 42 x 5	44. 31 x 8	45. 84 x 6

Benita borrowed money from her dad to buy a CD player. She agreed to pay him $9 a month for two years. How much will Benita pay her dad?

_____

Multiplication

Sometimes you must multiply by a factor that contains two or more digits. Then you have to write partial products. The partial products must be written in the correct columns before they are added.

Example: Find the product of 27 and 16.

Step 1:

$$\begin{array}{r} {}^{4}27 \\ \times\,16 \\ \hline 162 \end{array}$$ $6 \times 27 = 162$

Step 2:

$$\begin{array}{r} 27 \\ \times\,16 \\ \hline 162 \\ 27 \\ \hline 432 \end{array}$$

162 Partial Product
27   Partial Product
432 Product

Find these products. Check your answers.

1. $\begin{array}{r}25\\ \times\,25\\ \hline\end{array}$	2. $\begin{array}{r}34\\ \times\,13\\ \hline\end{array}$	3. $\begin{array}{r}73\\ \times\,23\\ \hline\end{array}$	4. $\begin{array}{r}82\\ \times\,47\\ \hline\end{array}$	5. $\begin{array}{r}42\\ \times\,29\\ \hline\end{array}$	6. $\begin{array}{r}91\\ \times\,68\\ \hline\end{array}$
7. $\begin{array}{r}42\\ \times\,28\\ \hline\end{array}$	8. $\begin{array}{r}45\\ \times\,43\\ \hline\end{array}$	9. $\begin{array}{r}53\\ \times\,57\\ \hline\end{array}$	10. $\begin{array}{r}56\\ \times\,64\\ \hline\end{array}$	11. $\begin{array}{r}68\\ \times\,69\\ \hline\end{array}$	12. $\begin{array}{r}85\\ \times\,23\\ \hline\end{array}$
13. $\begin{array}{r}232\\ \times\,52\\ \hline\end{array}$	14. $\begin{array}{r}541\\ \times\,39\\ \hline\end{array}$	15. $\begin{array}{r}181\\ \times\,57\\ \hline\end{array}$	16. $\begin{array}{r}193\\ \times\,12\\ \hline\end{array}$	17. $\begin{array}{r}182\\ \times\,48\\ \hline\end{array}$	18. $\begin{array}{r}370\\ \times\,22\\ \hline\end{array}$
19. $\begin{array}{r}142\\ \times\,22\\ \hline\end{array}$	20. $\begin{array}{r}331\\ \times\,59\\ \hline\end{array}$	21. $\begin{array}{r}801\\ \times\,39\\ \hline\end{array}$	22. $\begin{array}{r}442\\ \times\,33\\ \hline\end{array}$	23. $\begin{array}{r}515\\ \times\,23\\ \hline\end{array}$	24. $\begin{array}{r}463\\ \times\,85\\ \hline\end{array}$
25. $\begin{array}{r}231\\ \times\,442\\ \hline\end{array}$	26. $\begin{array}{r}182\\ \times\,382\\ \hline\end{array}$	27. $\begin{array}{r}514\\ \times\,772\\ \hline\end{array}$	28. $\begin{array}{r}555\\ \times\,131\\ \hline\end{array}$	29. $\begin{array}{r}622\\ \times\,485\\ \hline\end{array}$	30. $\begin{array}{r}778\\ \times\,662\\ \hline\end{array}$

Multiplying with Zero

Multiplying with zero is simple because zero times any number equals zero.

When the multiplier, or bottom number, in a multiplication problem has a zero on the right, you can write this zero in the product. If there is more than one zero on the right side of the multiplier, put the same number of zeros in the product.

Examples: Find the product of 27 and 80.

Factors ➤ 27
            x 80   **Multiplier**
         2,160   **Product**
Write the zero in the product.
Multiply by 8.

Find the product of 245 and 300.

Factors ➤ 245
            x 300   **Multiplier**
        73,500   **Product**
Write two zeros in the product.
Multiply by 3.

Find the products. Check your answers.

1. 383 x 20	2. 442 x 50	3. 723 x 30	4. 822 x 40	5. 227 x 90
6. 342 x 50	7. 522 x 60	8. 208 x 70	9. 551 x 30	10. 639 x 20
11. 532 x 600	12. 844 x 900	13. 394 x 700	14. 745 x 400	15. 641 x 500
16. 409 x 400	17. 559 x 500	18. 711 x 300	19. 603 x 300	20. 490 x 700
21. 252 x 200	22. 603 x 400	23. 434 x 800	24. 763 x 300	25. 307 x 500
26. 620 x 600	27. 944 x 500	28. 805 x 900	29. 750 x 700	30. 623 x 300

 Use the x key on a calculator to find the product.
Pencils are packed in boxes of 500. How many pencils
are needed to fill 712 boxes? _____

Zeros in the Multiplier

If you find a zero in the middle of a multiplier, you can take advantage of a mathematical shortcut. Write just one zero as the partial product and leave out the other zeros. Be sure to line up the next partial product correctly.

Example: Multiply 432 by 203.

Method A

```
    432
  x 203
  1,296
```
These zeros can be omitted. **00**0
```
    864
  87,696
```

Method B

```
    432
  x 203
  1,296
  8,640
  87,696
```

Multiply. Check your answers.

1. 235 x 304	2. 641 x 402	3. 728 x 204	4. 675 x 103	5. 691 x 601
6. 482 x 303	7. 607 x 406	8. 569 x 602	9. 362 x 909	10. 886 x 101
11. 366 x 703	12. 885 x 702	13. 969 x 209	14. 686 x 109	15. 772 x 705
16. 4,501 x 7,010	17. 3,040 x 5,500	18. 7,980 x 3,006	19. 6,774 x 4,050	20. 5,067 x 3,000
21. 1,003 x 1,003	22. 2,010 x 4,903	23. 3,099 x 2,040	24. 9,004 x 8,008	25. 9,304 x 8,030

Multiplication Practice

 Multiply. Check your answers.

1.
72	57	96	84	59	57	46
x 2	x 4	x 6	x 1	x 9	x 8	x 0

2.
344	567	587	953	629	234	345
x 6	x 7	x 4	x 2	x 3	x 8	x 2

3.
45	56	74	78	35	97	75
x 57	x 45	x 90	x 52	x 12	x 44	x 35

4.
307	405	902	603	505	806	908
x 5	x 6	x 2	x 6	x 3	x 7	x 9

5.
60	30	59	280	904	203	821
x 24	x 15	x 70	x 38	x 25	x 84	x 70

6.
905	820	604	920	207	104	590
x 45	x 29	x 52	x 63	x 41	x 11	x 92

7.
735	856	937	246	670	852	955
x 12	x 75	x 32	x 51	x 37	x 20	x 16

8.
531	892	175	416	732	809	512
x 178	x 219	x 354	x 150	x 332	x 299	x 152

9.
227	981	425	183	239	731	208
x 103	x 370	x 620	x 355	x 414	x 882	x 266

 The Community Drama Club sold tickets for its spring play. Twenty-six women members each sold 54 tickets. Thirty-two men members each sold 40 tickets. How many tickets were sold for the play? _____

Dividing Whole Numbers

Division is the opposite of multiplication.

Example: 8 ÷ 2 = ?   Write this: $\dfrac{4}{2\overline{)8}}$ **Quotient**
                                                              Dividend

                                                                    Divisor

When you divide, place the digits correctly in the quotient.

Example: 84 ÷ 7 = ?

$$\begin{array}{r} 1 \\ 7\overline{)84} \\ \underline{7} \end{array}$$

Because
7 x 1 = 7

$$\begin{array}{r} 1 \\ 7\overline{)84} \\ \underline{-7} \\ 14 \end{array}$$

8 – 7 = 1
Bring down the 4.

$$\begin{array}{r} 12 \\ 7\overline{)84} \\ \underline{-7} \\ 14 \\ \underline{-14} \\ 0 \end{array}$$

7 x 2 = 14 with 0
as a remainder.

 Divide. Check your answers.

1. $4\overline{)12}$ 2. $6\overline{)18}$ 3. $5\overline{)25}$ 4. $9\overline{)45}$ 5. $8\overline{)72}$

6. $8\overline{)64}$ 7. $7\overline{)56}$ 8. $3\overline{)48}$ 9. $2\overline{)48}$ 10. $6\overline{)66}$

11. $4\overline{)48}$ 12. $9\overline{)81}$ 13. $6\overline{)42}$ 14. $8\overline{)88}$ 15. $4\overline{)28}$

16. $7\overline{)77}$ 17. $4\overline{)52}$ 18. $5\overline{)60}$ 19. $7\overline{)84}$ 20. $6\overline{)78}$

21. $4\overline{)56}$ 22. $5\overline{)70}$ 23. $8\overline{)96}$ 24. $6\overline{)90}$ 25. $4\overline{)64}$

26. $9\overline{)126}$ 27. $8\overline{)104}$ 28. $6\overline{)114}$ 29. $5\overline{)115}$ 30. $6\overline{)126}$

Division with Remainders

The quotient (answer) of a division problem may not always be a whole number.

In 69, there are 2 sets of 28 and 13 left over. The answer is written 2 R13.

In 486, there are 14 sets of 33 and 24 left over. The answer is written as 14 R24.

Examples:

$$2\frac{13}{28} \quad \text{Remainder} \atop \text{Divisor}$$
$$28)\overline{69}$$
$$\underline{-56}$$
$$13 \quad \text{Remainder}$$

The remainder is always less than the dividend.

$$\frac{24}{33} \quad \text{Remainder} \atop \text{Divisor}$$
$$14$$
$$33)\overline{486}$$
$$\underline{33}$$
$$156$$
$$\underline{-132} \quad \text{Remainder}$$
$$24$$

■ Divide.

1. $23)\overline{68}$

2. $48)\overline{179}$

3. $62)\overline{785}$

4. $28)\overline{562}$

5. $86)\overline{695}$

6. $92)\overline{185}$

7. $20)\overline{77}$

8. $32)\overline{298}$

9. $31)\overline{689}$

10. $15)\overline{677}$

11. $39)\overline{86}$

12. $32)\overline{475}$

13. $56)\overline{784}$

14. $82)\overline{693}$

15. $63)\overline{772}$

16. $72)\overline{862}$

17. $72)\overline{6,912}$

18. $35)\overline{4,192}$

19. $38)\overline{1,093}$

20. $23)\overline{6,219}$

Eric gathered 161 eggs and packed them in cartons of twelve. How many cartons did he fill? Were any eggs left over?

_____

Applications with Division

Example: Oscar needs $192 for a new VCR. He can save $16 a month. How many months will he need to save $192?

Solution: Divide $192 by $16.

```
         12
$16)$192
      16
      32
      32
       0
```

Oscar will need 12 months to save $192.

Solve these problems by dividing and write your answers on the lines.

_____ 1. Leonardo uses 7,296 pounds of sugar each year in his bake shop. How many pounds of sugar does he use per month?

_____ 2. The scouts of Troop 109 collected 3,175 aluminum cans. Each scout collected the same number of cans. There were 25 scouts. How many cans did each scout collect?

_____ 3. Marlena drove her car 12,852 miles last year. How many miles did she average a month?

_____ 4. Sam's new car gets 38 miles per gallon. How many gallons will he need for a 6,232-mile trip?

_____ 5. Bill's old car gets 17 miles per gallon. How many gallons of gas will he need for a 493-mile trip?

_____ 6. Rebecca saved $728 for a down payment on a new computer. She saved $14 each week. How many weeks did it take her to save the down payment?

_____ 7. Felix slept 224 hours in the last four weeks. How many hours per week did he sleep? How many hours per day did he sleep?

_____ 8. In Burnsville, 1,680 households get the morning newspaper. The delivery routes are equally divided among 12 carriers. How many papers does each carrier deliver?

_____ 9. Mrs. Clark planted 588 tulips in 14 equal rows. How many tulips were in each row?

_____ 10. The warehouse received a shipment of 435 computers and 240 printers. Each of the company's 5 stores receive an equal amount of inventory. How many computers and printers will be shipped to each store?

UNIT 2 *WHOLE NUMBERS*   25

Practice with Combined Operations

A Solve these problems.

_____   **1.** Divide the sum of 485 and 632 by 28.

_____   **2.** Subtract the sum of 28, 16, 5, and 12 from 100.

_____   **3.** Divide the sum of 40, 192, 102, 311, and 30 by the sum of 12, 2, and 11.

_____   **4.** Multiply the sum of 2, 10, and 4 by the quotient of 10 ÷ 2.

_____   **5.** Divide the sum of 14 and 211 by 5.

_____   **6.** Multiply the product of 3 x 17 by the quotient of 32 ÷ 8.

B Read each item. Write the order of operations—addition, subtraction, multiplication, or division—you would perform to obtain the answers. Then solve the problem.

_____   **7.** Tomas spent $19 at the gas station; $78 at the grocery store; and $12 at the cleaners. His paycheck was $250. Does he have enough money left to buy a jacket that costs $112?

_____   **8.** Lin is a florist. She has 80 roses, 120 daisies, and 300 carnations. She wants to make mixed bouquets of 10 flowers each. How many bouquets can she make?

_____   **9.** Ed picked 27 apples from each of the 30 trees in his orchard. He used 420 apples to make pies for a local bakery. How many apples did Ed have left?

_____   **10.** Cans of soup are packed in cases of 144 cans. Super Foods ordered 10 cases of soup. One dozen of the cans were dented and were not sold. How many cans of soup were sold?

Proficiency Test 1

 Circle the correct answer.

1. 4038
    − 1473
    - a. 3,445
    - b. 3,465
    - c. 2,565
    - d. 3,565

2. 2435
    3028
    483
    + 1658
    - a. 7,604
    - b. 7,594
    - c. 7,694
    - d. 7,504

3. The numeral for seven hundred thousand, twelve is
    - a. 712,000
    - b. 700,012
    - c. 700,100,012
    - d. 7,012

4. 2354
    × 18
    - a. 43,372
    - b. 42,372
    - c. 42,382
    - d. 21,186

5. What is 28,746 rounded to the nearest thousand?
    - a. 28,000
    - b. 29,000
    - c. 28,400
    - d. 28,500

6. 1728 ÷ 36 =
    - a. 46
    - b. 47
    - c. 48
    - d. 49

7. What is the place value of the underlined digit in 1̲7,248?
    - a. millions
    - b. ten-thousands
    - c. hundreds
    - d. thousands

8. 327
    × 46
    - a. 15,042
    - b. 14,942
    - c. 15,142
    - d. 3,270

9. The number 8,411 rounded to the nearest hundred is
    - a. 8,410
    - b. 8,500
    - c. 8,000
    - d. 8,400

10. You spend $6.38. What change should you get from ten dollars?
    - a. $3.72
    - b. $4.72
    - c. $3.62
    - d. $4.62

11. The numeral for eight hundred eight is
    - a. 80
    - b. 88
    - c. 808
    - d. 800

12. To find the cost of 8 comic books, each costing $1.75, you would
    - a. add
    - b. subtract
    - c. multiply
    - d. divide

13. 500 + 4 + 1,260 + 20 =
    - a. 1,784
    - b. 1,874
    - c. 3,748
    - d. 1,334

14. What is 3,287 rounded to the nearest hundred?
    - a. 328
    - b. 3,280
    - c. 3,300
    - d. 3,288

15. 6,009 − 341 =
    - a. 5,768
    - b. 6,768
    - c. 5,858
    - d. 5,668

16. 264 × 102
    - a. 3,188
    - b. 26,928
    - c. 7,920
    - d. 27,028

17. 11)214
    - a. 19 R6
    - b. 19 R5
    - c. 19
    - d. 18 R16

18. The number 21,129 rounded to the nearest ten is
    - a. 21,130
    - b. 21,120
    - c. 21,100
    - d. 21,010

19. What is the product of 2 × the sum of 36, 46, 52, 43, and 48?
    - a. 225
    - b. 450
    - c. 220
    - d. 400

20. 563 + 12 + 378 =
    - a. 953
    - b. 1,061
    - c. 1,861
    - d. 2,141

Introduction to Fractions

A fraction is a number that is less than 1. These numbers are fractions:

$$\frac{1}{2} \qquad \frac{3}{4} \qquad \frac{5}{8} \qquad \frac{15}{63}$$

A fraction is part of a whole. There are two parts to a fraction: the numerator and the denominator. The *denominator* tells how many parts the whole is divided into. The *numerator* names a certain number of those parts. The numerator is the number above the fraction line. The denominator is the number below the fraction line.

Numerators: $\frac{1}{}$ $\qquad$ $\frac{3}{}$ $\qquad$ $\frac{5}{}$ $\qquad$ $\frac{15}{}$
Denominators: $\frac{}{2}$ $\qquad$ $\frac{}{4}$ $\qquad$ $\frac{}{8}$ $\qquad$ $\frac{}{63}$

Example: $\dfrac{1}{2}$ means 1 part.

means the whole is divided into 2 parts.

Because a fraction is actually part of a whole, it is easy to picture it. Think of a pizza and one hungry student. When the pizza arrived, it was cut into 4 equal pieces. But now, only 3 pieces are left. The 4 is the denominator, or bottom number. It says that the whole pizza was cut into 4 parts. The 3 is the numerator, or top number. It says that there are 3 parts left. Therefore, the fraction that describes what we see here is $\frac{3}{4}$ of a pizza.

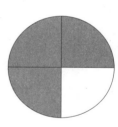

◼ Write fractions for the following.

1. 6 cars; 3 are blue _____

2. 10 CDs; 3 are rap music _____

3. 12 pieces of fruit; 2 are bananas _____

4. 13 people; 2 are women _____

5. 10 boys; 3 play soccer _____

6. 9 books; 1 is a paperback _____

7. 7 cats; 5 are black _____

8. 40 athletes; 10 are swimmers _____

Understanding Fractions

You can understand fractions by looking at other kinds of figures.

Look at this figure.

To determine the fraction that this figure represents, follow these steps:

1. Count the total number of blocks.
   This number is the denominator.
   Here the total is 6 blocks.

2. Count the total number of shaded blocks.
   This number is the numerator.
   Here the total is 2 shaded blocks.
   Therefore, the fraction that represents this figure is $\frac{2}{6}$.

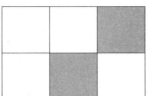

Write the fraction that represents each of these figures.

1.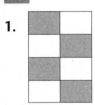

   _____

2.

   _____

3.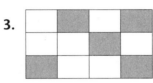

   _____

4.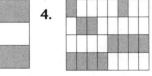

   _____

5.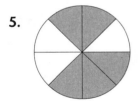

   _____

6.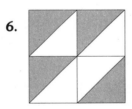

   _____

7.

   _____

8.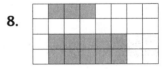

   _____

9.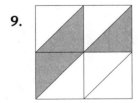

   _____

10.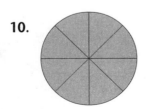

    _____

11.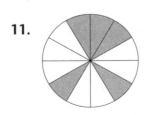

    _____

12.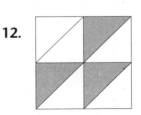

    _____

Shading Fractional Parts

This figure has a total of 16 parts. Five parts are shaded. This figure represents the fraction $\frac{5}{16}$.

$\frac{5}{16}$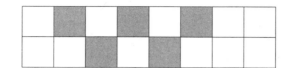

A Shade each figure to represent the given fraction.

1. $\frac{2}{3}$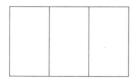

2. $\frac{15}{16}$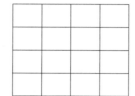

3. $\frac{5}{8}$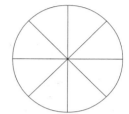

4. $\frac{3}{8}$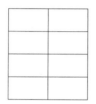

5. $\frac{5}{12}$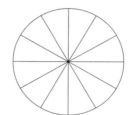

6. $\frac{8}{18}$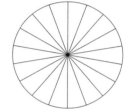

7. $\frac{10}{36}$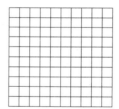

8. $\frac{9}{20}$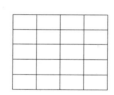

9. $\frac{6}{32}$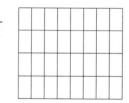

10. $\frac{7}{10}$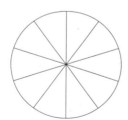

11. $\frac{15}{24}$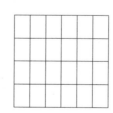

12. $\frac{11}{16}$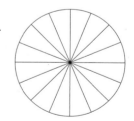

B Draw and shade figures to show $\frac{2}{10}$, $\frac{1}{4}$, $\frac{3}{13}$, and $\frac{10}{20}$.

Word Names for Fractions

There are special rules that you use when writing or reading fractions.

Rule 1:   Read or write the numerator first. Say or write it just as you would a whole number.

Rule 2:   Read or write the denominator second. Denominators are written or read with special endings. These endings are the same ones you would use to read a numbered street name. For example, 5th Avenue is read and correctly written as Fifth Avenue.

If we use these rules:

$\dfrac{5}{7}$ The numerator is read and written as "five."

The denominator is read and written as "sevenths."

Therefore, the fraction is read and written as "five sevenths."

Example: $\dfrac{6}{11}$ is read and written as "six elevenths."

DENOMINATOR SPELLING CHART				
half	third	fourth	fifth	sixth
seventh	eighth	ninth	tenth	eleventh
twelfth	thirteenth	fourteenth	fifteenth	sixteenth
seventeenth	eighteenth	nineteenth	twentieth	thirtieth
fortieth	fiftieth	sixtieth	seventieth	eightieth
ninetieth	hundredth			

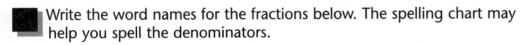 Write the word names for the fractions below. The spelling chart may help you spell the denominators.

1. $\dfrac{22}{80}$ _____

2. $\dfrac{12}{60}$ _____

3. $\dfrac{2}{17}$ _____

4. $\dfrac{18}{27}$ _____

5. $\dfrac{5}{90}$ _____

6. $\dfrac{70}{100}$ _____

7. $\dfrac{8}{30}$ _____

8. $\dfrac{17}{70}$ _____

9. $\dfrac{55}{69}$ _____

10. $\dfrac{1}{99}$ _____

11. $\dfrac{34}{48}$ _____

12. $\dfrac{7}{100}$ _____

Expressing Fractions in Higher Terms

Many operations in math require raising fractions to higher terms. To raise a fraction to higher terms, multiply the numerator and denominator by the same number.

Example: Write $\frac{7}{8}$ in higher terms with a new denominator of 40.

Step 1: Multiply the numerator by 5.
$7 \times 5 = 35$

Step 2: Multiply the denominator by 5, the multiplier.
$8 \times 5 = 40$

Step 3: $\frac{7}{8} \times \frac{5}{5} = \frac{35}{40}$

$\frac{35}{40}$ is the new fraction.

Example: Write $\frac{5}{7}$ in higher terms with a new denominator of 56.

Step 1: Find the multiplier by dividing 56 by 7.
$\frac{5}{7} = \frac{?}{56}$

Step 2: $56 \div 7 = 8$; therefore, 8 is the multiplier. Multiply both the numerator and denominator by the same number.
$\frac{5}{7} \times \frac{8}{8} = \frac{40}{56}$

Step 3: $\frac{40}{56}$ is the new fraction.

Write these fractions in higher terms.

1. $\frac{5}{11} = \frac{}{33}$

2. $\frac{6}{9} = \frac{}{27}$

3. $\frac{4}{5} = \frac{}{40}$

4. $\frac{6}{13} = \frac{}{39}$

5. $\frac{6}{12} = \frac{}{144}$

6. $\frac{4}{12} = \frac{}{48}$

7. $\frac{8}{9} = \frac{}{36}$

8. $\frac{3}{7} = \frac{}{28}$

9. $\frac{7}{11} = \frac{}{44}$

10. $\frac{11}{12} = \frac{}{156}$

11. $\frac{10}{13} = \frac{}{52}$

12. $\frac{8}{9} = \frac{}{72}$

13. $\frac{2}{9} = \frac{}{90}$

14. $\frac{7}{9} = \frac{}{54}$

15. $\frac{12}{15} = \frac{}{60}$

16. $\frac{23}{24} = \frac{}{48}$

17. $\frac{7}{8} = \frac{}{56}$

18. $\frac{2}{5} = \frac{}{60}$

19. $\frac{5}{8} = \frac{}{64}$

20. $\frac{6}{16} = \frac{}{64}$

21. $\frac{11}{12} = \frac{}{72}$

22. $\frac{3}{5} = \frac{}{55}$

23. $\frac{1}{8} = \frac{}{88}$

24. $\frac{3}{4} = \frac{}{100}$

25. $\frac{10}{21} = \frac{}{84}$

26. $\frac{5}{6} = \frac{}{30}$

27. $\frac{9}{11} = \frac{}{44}$

28. $\frac{3}{7} = \frac{}{21}$

29. $\frac{7}{12} = \frac{}{36}$

30. $\frac{5}{9} = \frac{}{45}$

Gloria, Meg, and Nancy participated in the Health Walk-a-thon. Gloria walked $6\frac{7}{9}$ miles, Meg walked $6\frac{32}{40}$ miles, and Nancy walked $6\frac{14}{18}$ miles. Which two girls walked the same number of miles?

_____

Expressing Fractions in Lowest Terms
Lesson 6

Expressing fractions in lower terms is the opposite of raising fractions to higher terms. To raise fractions, we multiply. To lower fractions, we divide the numerator and denominator by the same number. Use the greatest number that will divide both.

Example: Express $\frac{14}{18}$ in lowest terms.

Step 1: Divide the numerator by 2.
$14 \div 2 = 7$

Step 2: Divide the denominator by 2.
$18 \div 2 = 9$

Step 3: $\frac{14}{18} = \frac{7}{9}$

$\frac{7}{9}$ is the new fraction.

Example: Express $\frac{16}{20}$ in lowest terms.

Step 1: Divide the numerator by 4.
$16 \div 4 = 4$

Step 2: Divide the denominator by 4.
$20 \div 4 = 5$

Step 3: $\frac{16}{20} = \frac{4}{5}$

$\frac{4}{5}$ is the new fraction.

 Express these fractions in lowest terms.

1. $\frac{2}{10} =$ 2. $\frac{5}{25} =$ 3. $\frac{20}{30} =$ 4. $\frac{30}{40} =$ 5. $\frac{60}{66} =$

6. $\frac{12}{24} =$ 7. $\frac{7}{28} =$ 8. $\frac{9}{36} =$ 9. $\frac{8}{24} =$ 10. $\frac{18}{27} =$

11. $\frac{12}{28} =$ 12. $\frac{16}{40} =$ 13. $\frac{22}{40} =$ 14. $\frac{6}{22} =$ 15. $\frac{9}{45} =$

16. $\frac{8}{20} =$ 17. $\frac{63}{72} =$ 18. $\frac{18}{24} =$ 19. $\frac{50}{60} =$ 20. $\frac{10}{100} =$

21. $\frac{12}{42} =$ 22. $\frac{22}{121} =$ 23. $\frac{12}{132} =$ 24. $\frac{17}{51} =$ 25. $\frac{9}{21} =$

26. $\frac{14}{35} =$ 27. $\frac{32}{64} =$ 28. $\frac{28}{44} =$ 29. $\frac{50}{190} =$ 30. $\frac{22}{26} =$

31. $\frac{15}{80} =$ 32. $\frac{16}{80} =$ 33. $\frac{12}{84} =$ 34. $\frac{33}{121} =$ 35. $\frac{6}{42} =$

36. $\frac{8}{72} =$ 37. $\frac{51}{102} =$ 38. $\frac{25}{75} =$ 39. $\frac{30}{100} =$ 40. $\frac{56}{64} =$

Mixed Numbers to Improper Fractions

Mixed numbers are numbers that contain a whole number and a fraction. $5\frac{2}{3}$ is a mixed number.

Sometimes, math problems that contain mixed numbers have to be changed to a new form before you complete the mathematics involved. This new form is called an improper fraction. An improper fraction is more than 1. $\frac{15}{3}$, $\frac{8}{6}$, $\frac{30}{27}$ are improper fractions.

An improper fraction has a larger number in the numerator than in the denominator.

Example: Express $5\frac{2}{3}$ as an improper fraction.

To change a mixed number to an improper fraction, follow these steps:

Step 1:   Multiply the denominator by the whole number. $3 \times 5 = 15$

Step 2:   Add the product to the numerator. $15 + 2 = 17$

Step 3:   Write the sum over the denominator. $\frac{17}{3}$

Write these mixed numbers as improper fractions.

1. $2\frac{1}{2} =$ 2. $5\frac{1}{3} =$ 3. $7\frac{2}{3} =$ 4. $6\frac{3}{5} =$

5. $3\frac{2}{3} =$ 6. $4\frac{1}{5} =$ 7. $5\frac{2}{7} =$ 8. $6\frac{1}{2} =$

9. $5\frac{2}{5} =$ 10. $8\frac{1}{7} =$ 11. $8\frac{3}{9} =$ 12. $3\frac{2}{12} =$

13. $6\frac{2}{11} =$ 14. $14\frac{1}{2} =$ 15. $9\frac{3}{10} =$ 16. $12\frac{2}{12} =$

17. $6\frac{7}{10} =$ 18. $8\frac{5}{11} =$ 19. $1\frac{3}{5} =$ 20. $7\frac{4}{5} =$

  A carpenter cut a board that was $\frac{3}{4}$ foot long from a board that was $5\frac{1}{4}$ feet long. How long was the remaining piece of wood?

_____

Improper Fractions to Mixed Numbers

In some mathematical problems, you have to change improper fractions to mixed numbers.

Example: Rename $\frac{16}{5}$ as a mixed number.

In order to change an improper fraction to a mixed number, follow these steps:

Step 1: Divide the numerator by the denominator.

Step 2: Put the remainder over the denominator to make a fraction.

Step 3: Write your answer as a mixed number. $\frac{16}{5} = 3\frac{1}{5}$

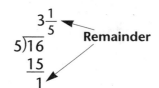

Examples: $\frac{18}{3} = 6$ $\qquad$ $\frac{25}{3} = 8\frac{1}{3}$ $\qquad$ $\frac{32}{7} = 4\frac{4}{7}$

■ Rename these improper fractions as mixed numbers.

1. $\frac{28}{11} =$ $\qquad$ 2. $\frac{38}{2} =$ $\qquad$ 3. $\frac{39}{2} =$ $\qquad$ 4. $\frac{5}{3} =$ $\qquad$ 5. $\frac{19}{5} =$

6. $\frac{16}{5} =$ $\qquad$ 7. $\frac{29}{8} =$ $\qquad$ 8. $\frac{53}{11} =$ $\qquad$ 9. $\frac{34}{10} =$ $\qquad$ 10. $\frac{37}{5} =$

11. $\frac{42}{7} =$ $\qquad$ 12. $\frac{46}{7} =$ $\qquad$ 13. $\frac{80}{10} =$ $\qquad$ 14. $\frac{53}{10} =$ $\qquad$ 15. $\frac{25}{7} =$

16. $\frac{22}{4} =$ $\qquad$ 17. $\frac{32}{15} =$ $\qquad$ 18. $\frac{29}{17} =$ $\qquad$ 19. $\frac{36}{9} =$ $\qquad$ 20. $\frac{51}{17} =$

21. $\frac{63}{8} =$ $\qquad$ 22. $\frac{59}{12} =$ $\qquad$ 23. $\frac{40}{6} =$ $\qquad$ 24. $\frac{72}{9} =$ $\qquad$ 25. $\frac{71}{10} =$

26. $\frac{35}{6} =$ $\qquad$ 27. $\frac{81}{9} =$ $\qquad$ 28. $\frac{43}{13} =$ $\qquad$ 29. $\frac{31}{11} =$ $\qquad$ 30. $\frac{7}{2} =$

Renaming Mixed Numbers with Improper Fractions   Lesson 9

Sometimes, when you work a mathematics problem, you get an answer that has a mixed number with an improper fraction. Remember, an improper fraction is more than 1. You may have to rename the fraction to a whole number and improper fraction.

Example: Rename $13\frac{7}{2}$.

Step 1:   Think of the mixed number with an improper fraction as the sum of two parts of the answer. Separate the two parts. $13\frac{7}{2} = 13 + \frac{7}{2}$

Step 2:   Rename the improper fraction. $\frac{7}{2} = 7 \div 2 = 3\frac{1}{2}$

Step 3:   Add the parts. $13 + 3\frac{1}{2} = 16\frac{1}{2}$

$$13\frac{7}{2} = 16\frac{1}{2}$$

Rename these mixed numbers as whole numbers with proper fractions.

1. $13\frac{5}{2} =$

2. $16\frac{15}{5} =$

3. $5\frac{6}{3} =$

4. $11\frac{15}{10} =$

5. $39\frac{12}{10} =$

6   $15\frac{15}{7} =$

7. $28\frac{6}{5} =$

8. $13\frac{7}{6} =$

9. $26\frac{11}{5} =$

10. $14\frac{18}{7} =$

11. $19\frac{3}{2} =$

12. $23\frac{5}{4} =$

13. $33\frac{8}{6} =$

14. $2\frac{7}{5} =$

15. $13\frac{17}{16} =$

16. $8\frac{16}{7} =$

17. $15\frac{8}{2} =$

18. $8\frac{9}{3} =$

19. $9\frac{13}{10} =$

20. $71\frac{22}{10} =$

21. $9\frac{10}{2} =$

22. $12\frac{8}{7} =$

23. $16\frac{11}{7} =$

24. $6\frac{9}{8} =$

A baker had $23\frac{28}{14}$ pies left at the end of the day. How many pies did he have left?

_____

Adding Fractions with Like Denominators

Adding fractions and mixed numbers is much like adding whole numbers. You add the whole numbers, add the numerators, and keep the same denominator.

Examples:

$$2\frac{2}{5}$$
$$+4\frac{1}{5}$$
$$\overline{6\frac{3}{5}}$$

Step 1: Add the whole-number portions.
$2 + 4 = 6$

Step 2: Add the numerators. $2 + 1 = 3$

Step 3: The new numerator is 3.
The denominator remains the same, 5.

$$3\frac{5}{6}$$
$$+5\frac{4}{6}$$
$$\overline{8\frac{9}{6}} = 9\frac{1}{2}$$

Step 1: Add the whole-number portions.
$3 + 5 = 8$

Step 2: Add the numerators. $5 + 4 = 9$

Step 3: The sum $8\frac{9}{6}$ can be renamed to $9\frac{1}{2}$.

Add these fractions. Rename your answers in lowest terms.

1. $\frac{2}{7}$
$+\frac{3}{7}$

2. $\frac{5}{11}$
$+\frac{4}{11}$

3. $\frac{6}{13}$
$+\frac{8}{13}$

4. $5\frac{2}{15}$
$+6\frac{5}{15}$

5. $7\frac{7}{11}$
$+\frac{6}{11}$

6. $6\frac{7}{13}$
$+5\frac{3}{13}$

7. $9\frac{4}{13}$
$+10\frac{9}{13}$

8. $6\frac{2}{7}$
$+\frac{6}{7}$

9. $9\frac{1}{15}$
$+\frac{13}{15}$

10. $8\frac{2}{18}$
$+\frac{3}{18}$

11. $8\frac{1}{5}$
$+2\frac{4}{5}$

12. $7\frac{7}{16}$
$+1\frac{1}{16}$

13. $9\frac{2}{11}$
$+2\frac{5}{11}$

14. $5\frac{9}{12}$
$+\frac{2}{12}$

15. $8\frac{11}{15}$
$+3\frac{4}{15}$

Adding Fractions with Unlike Denominators

Adding fractions requires like, or common, denominators. If the denominators are not alike, then a common denominator must be found. Always consider the larger of the given denominators as a possible common denominator.

Hint: Try dividing the smaller denominator into the larger denominator. If the remainder is zero, then the larger denominator can be used as a common denominator.

Example: Add $2\frac{2}{7}$ and $5\frac{3}{28}$.

$$2\frac{2}{7}$$
$$+5\frac{3}{28}$$

Step 1: Find the least common multiple for the denominators 7 and 28. $28 \div 7 = 4$. The remainder is zero. Use 28 as the common denominator.

$$\frac{2}{7} \times \frac{4}{4} = \frac{8}{28}$$

Step 2: Raise the smaller fraction to higher terms with 28 as the new denominator.

$$2\frac{2}{7} = 2\frac{8}{28}$$

Step 3: Proceed with the addition. Add the numerators and the whole number parts.

$$+5\frac{3}{28} = 5\frac{3}{28}$$
$$\overline{7\frac{11}{28}}$$

■ Find the least common denominator and add. Express your answers in lowest terms.

1. $13\frac{4}{9}$
    $+2\frac{3}{36}$

2. $15\frac{1}{5}$
    $+6\frac{6}{25}$

3. $7\frac{2}{8}$
    $+\frac{1}{4}$

4. $5\frac{2}{18}$
    $+4\frac{5}{6}$

5. $28\frac{5}{32}$
    $+6\frac{2}{8}$

6. $2\frac{3}{13}$
    $+\frac{5}{52}$

7. $3\frac{4}{37}$
    $+5\frac{3}{74}$

8. $6\frac{5}{12}$
    $+4\frac{2}{3}$

9. $4\frac{2}{5}$
    $+3\frac{7}{15}$

10. $16\frac{5}{10}$
    $+8\frac{2}{30}$

11. $5\frac{6}{7}$
    $+4\frac{8}{42}$

12. $9\frac{6}{35}$
    $+8\frac{4}{7}$

13. $7\frac{5}{39}$
    $+\frac{1}{13}$

14. $38\frac{5}{36}$
    $+4\frac{3}{12}$

15. $3\frac{5}{18}$
    $+8\frac{5}{54}$

The Silvas were painting their house. Mr. Silva used $3\frac{1}{5}$ gallons of paint for the living room. Mrs. Silva used $2\frac{2}{3}$ gallons of paint for the dining room. How much paint did the Silvas use? _____

Using Least Common Multiples

Often, the fractions that you need to add have unlike denominators. You may not be able to find a common denominator in the problem. Then you need to use the least common multiple as the common denominator.

Example: Add $5\frac{3}{4}$ and $2\frac{1}{6}$.

Step 1: Find the least common multiple of 4 and 6.

The least common multiple is 12. Use 12 as the least common denominator.

The multiples of 4 are
(4, 8, **12**, 16, 20, 24, 28, 32.......)
The multiples of 6 are
(6, **12**, 18, 24, 30, 36.......)

Step 2: Raise the fractions to higher terms with 12 as the new denominator.

$$5\frac{3}{4} = 5\frac{9}{12}$$
$$+ 2\frac{1}{6} = 2\frac{2}{12}$$
$$\overline{\phantom{+ 2\frac{1}{6} = }7\frac{11}{12}}$$

 Add these fractions. Express your answers in lowest terms.

1. $5\frac{2}{7}$
    $+ 6\frac{4}{8}$

2. $6\frac{5}{6}$
    $+ 2\frac{3}{4}$

3. $39\frac{1}{2}$
    $+ 4\frac{3}{5}$

4. $5\frac{2}{7}$
    $+ 5\frac{3}{9}$

5. $6\frac{4}{8}$
    $+ 2\frac{1}{5}$

6. $4\frac{1}{6}$
    $+ 3\frac{5}{8}$

7. $8\frac{1}{3}$
    $+ 4\frac{1}{4}$

8. $8\frac{1}{6}$
    $+ 2\frac{2}{7}$

9. $4\frac{2}{15}$
    $+ 2\frac{1}{2}$

10. $16\frac{9}{11}$
    $+ \frac{1}{3}$

11. $3\frac{2}{9}$
    $+ 2\frac{1}{5}$

12. $4\frac{2}{5}$
    $+ 2\frac{3}{11}$

13. $16\frac{5}{11}$
    $+ 4\frac{3}{4}$

14. $3\frac{1}{5}$
    $+ \frac{3}{10}$

15. $2\frac{3}{5}$
    $+ 4\frac{1}{8}$

16. $5\frac{1}{6}$
    $+ 2\frac{3}{4}$

17. $9\frac{5}{6}$
    $+ 4\frac{1}{5}$

18. $4\frac{1}{2}$
    $+ 3\frac{2}{3}$

19. $8\frac{1}{7}$
    $+ \frac{5}{8}$

20. $4\frac{2}{9}$
    $+ 5\frac{1}{5}$

Subtracting with Like Denominators

You need like denominators to subtract fractions or mixed numbers. If the denominators are alike, you subtract the whole numbers and the numerators. You keep the same common denominator for your answer. You may need to rename your answer in lowest terms.

Example:

$$\begin{array}{r} 12\frac{8}{9} \\ -\ 10\frac{7}{9} \\ \hline 2\frac{1}{9} \end{array}$$

Since the denominators are the same, subtract the numerators.
$8 - 7 = 1$

■ Subtract. Express your answers in lowest terms.

1. $\begin{array}{r} 5\frac{7}{8} \\ -\ 4\frac{5}{8} \\ \hline \end{array}$

2. $\begin{array}{r} 8\frac{5}{12} \\ -\ 2\frac{3}{12} \\ \hline \end{array}$

3. $\begin{array}{r} 12\frac{11}{16} \\ -\ 3\frac{5}{16} \\ \hline \end{array}$

4. $\begin{array}{r} 8\frac{36}{40} \\ -\ 2\frac{11}{40} \\ \hline \end{array}$

5. $\begin{array}{r} 9\frac{2}{10} \\ -\ 3\frac{1}{10} \\ \hline \end{array}$

6. $\begin{array}{r} 8\frac{10}{32} \\ -\ 2\frac{8}{32} \\ \hline \end{array}$

7. $\begin{array}{r} 36\frac{21}{45} \\ -\ 8\frac{9}{45} \\ \hline \end{array}$

8. $\begin{array}{r} 30\frac{26}{50} \\ -\ 8\frac{11}{50} \\ \hline \end{array}$

9. $\begin{array}{r} 39\frac{21}{52} \\ -\ 6\frac{7}{52} \\ \hline \end{array}$

10. $\begin{array}{r} 38\frac{10}{11} \\ -\ 4\frac{4}{11} \\ \hline \end{array}$

11. $\begin{array}{r} 65\frac{23}{24} \\ -\ 5\frac{21}{24} \\ \hline \end{array}$

12. $\begin{array}{r} 18\frac{15}{20} \\ -\ 6\frac{11}{20} \\ \hline \end{array}$

13. $\begin{array}{r} 4\frac{6}{8} \\ -\ 2\frac{1}{8} \\ \hline \end{array}$

14. $\begin{array}{r} 15\frac{16}{17} \\ -\ 10\frac{6}{17} \\ \hline \end{array}$

15. $\begin{array}{r} 1\frac{11}{12} \\ -\ \frac{5}{12} \\ \hline \end{array}$

16. $\begin{array}{r} 24\frac{25}{70} \\ -\ 5\frac{20}{70} \\ \hline \end{array}$

17. $\begin{array}{r} 80\frac{12}{13} \\ -\ 11\frac{10}{13} \\ \hline \end{array}$

18. $\begin{array}{r} 6\frac{11}{45} \\ -\ 1\frac{7}{45} \\ \hline \end{array}$

19. $\begin{array}{r} 10\frac{17}{60} \\ -\ 8\frac{8}{60} \\ \hline \end{array}$

20. $\begin{array}{r} 18\frac{13}{57} \\ -\ 9\frac{11}{57} \\ \hline \end{array}$

 Aiko made $7\frac{6}{8}$ quarts of lemonade to serve at the family picnic. Her 5 cousins drank $2\frac{1}{8}$ quarts. How much lemonade was left for the rest of the family?

_____

Subtracting with Unlike Denominators

When you subtract fractions, the fractions have to have the same denominator.
If they don't, you have to find the least common denominator.

Example: From $15\frac{2}{3}$ subtract $5\frac{1}{8}$.

Step 1: Find the least common multiple of 3 and 8.
Step 2: Use 24 as the least common denominator.
Step 3: Raise the fractions to higher terms. Then subtract.

The least common multiple of 3 and 8 is 24.

$$15\frac{2}{3} = 15\frac{16}{24}$$
$$-5\frac{1}{8} = 5\frac{3}{24}$$
$$\overline{10\frac{13}{24}}$$

Subtract these fractions. Express your answers in lowest terms.

1. $\frac{7}{8}$ $-\frac{1}{6}$

2. $\frac{5}{10}$ $-\frac{1}{3}$

3. $\frac{3}{4}$ $-\frac{2}{9}$

4. $\frac{4}{7}$ $-\frac{1}{5}$

5. $\frac{5}{6}$ $-\frac{3}{8}$

6. $38\frac{4}{5}$ $-5\frac{3}{6}$

7. $5\frac{5}{5}$ $-2\frac{3}{8}$

8. $45\frac{5}{8}$ $-6\frac{1}{3}$

9. $45\frac{2}{3}$ -6

10. $18\frac{12}{15}$ $-\frac{1}{30}$

11. $6\frac{8}{11}$ $-4\frac{3}{22}$

12. $12\frac{4}{5}$ $-2\frac{1}{3}$

13. $10\frac{7}{11}$ $-5\frac{1}{33}$

14. $45\frac{12}{17}$ $-8\frac{1}{2}$

15. $8\frac{4}{7}$ $-\frac{2}{28}$

16. $39\frac{12}{19}$ $-4\frac{1}{3}$

17. $21\frac{5}{9}$ $-2\frac{1}{5}$

18. $28\frac{5}{7}$ $-9\frac{1}{4}$

19. $11\frac{15}{16}$ $-3\frac{1}{3}$

20. $23\frac{21}{22}$ $-5\frac{2}{5}$

21. $17\frac{5}{8}$ $-4\frac{1}{3}$

22. $12\frac{7}{10}$ $-6\frac{2}{3}$

23. $42\frac{3}{5}$ $-35\frac{3}{10}$

24. $21\frac{3}{8}$ $-9\frac{3}{20}$

25. $9\frac{5}{8}$ $-\frac{2}{6}$

Subtraction with Renaming

Sometimes, when you subtract with fractions, you have to rename the numbers. Sometimes you have to change whole numbers to mixed numbers. A *mixed number* is a whole number with a fraction. At other times, you have to change a mixed number to a mixed number with an improper fraction. An *improper fraction* is a fraction with a larger number in the numerator than in the denominator.

When you make these changes, keep this in mind: Each whole number can be changed into a fraction with a numerator and a denominator that are the same.

$1 = \boxed{\frac{1}{2}}\boxed{\frac{1}{2}} = \boxed{\frac{1}{3}}\boxed{\frac{1}{3}}\boxed{\frac{1}{3}} = \boxed{\frac{1}{4}}\boxed{\frac{1}{4}}\boxed{\frac{1}{4}}\boxed{\frac{1}{4}} = \boxed{\frac{1}{5}}\boxed{\frac{1}{5}}\boxed{\frac{1}{5}}\boxed{\frac{1}{5}}\boxed{\frac{1}{5}}$

$1 = \frac{2}{2} = \frac{3}{3} = \frac{4}{4} = \frac{5}{5}$

Example: Subtract $5\frac{7}{8}$ from 18.

Step 1: $18 = 17 + 1 =$ $17\frac{8}{8}$
(mixed number with an improper fraction)

Step 2: Subtract.

$$\begin{array}{r} 17\frac{8}{8} \\ -\ 5\frac{7}{8} \\ \hline 12\frac{1}{8} \end{array}$$

Example: Subtract $10\frac{3}{7}$ from $15\frac{1}{7}$.

Step 1: $15\frac{1}{7} = 14 + 1 + \frac{1}{7}$
$= 14 + \frac{7}{7} + \frac{1}{7} =$ $14\frac{8}{7}$
(mixed number with an improper fraction)

Step 2: Subtract.

$$\begin{array}{r} 14\frac{8}{7} \\ -\ 10\frac{3}{7} \\ \hline 4\frac{5}{7} \end{array}$$

Subtract these fractions. Express your answers in lowest terms.

1. $6\frac{5}{17} - 2\frac{8}{17}$
2. $16 - 4\frac{3}{5}$
3. $18\frac{1}{7} - 6\frac{5}{21}$
4. $8\frac{1}{4} - 3\frac{11}{36}$
5. $4 - 2\frac{8}{11}$
6. $19\frac{1}{8} - 5\frac{5}{6}$
7. $21\frac{2}{5} - 6\frac{4}{5}$
8. $8\frac{9}{11} - 2\frac{10}{11}$
9. $53\frac{2}{21} - 4\frac{5}{21}$
10. $56\frac{2}{10} - 6\frac{4}{9}$
11. $19\frac{2}{9} - 8\frac{3}{4}$
12. $15 - 8\frac{3}{21}$

Paul bought 18 yards of carpeting for his new office. The office was smaller than he had thought, so he used only $14\frac{2}{3}$ yards of carpet. How much carpet was left over? ____________

Multiplying Fractions

You multiply fractions by multiplying the numerators and then multiplying the denominators.

Example: $\dfrac{5}{6} \times \dfrac{1}{2} = ?$

$\dfrac{5}{6} \times \dfrac{1}{2} = \dfrac{5}{12}$ ◀— because 5 x 1 = 5
　　　　　　　　◀— because 6 x 2 = 12

Often, you can simplify the problem before multiplying.

Example: $\dfrac{4}{15} \times \dfrac{5}{7} = ?$

$\dfrac{4}{{}_{3}\cancel{15}} \times \dfrac{\cancel{5}^{1}}{7} = ?$ Divide the 15 and 5 by the common factor of 5. Then multiply.

$\dfrac{4}{3} \times \dfrac{1}{7} = \dfrac{4}{21}$ ◀— because 4 x 1 = 4
　　　　　　　　◀— because 3 x 7 = 21

■ Multiply. Express your answers in lowest terms.

1. $\dfrac{2}{11} \times \dfrac{5}{1} =$

2. $\dfrac{8}{13} \times \dfrac{26}{27} =$

3. $\dfrac{5}{16} \times \dfrac{8}{10} =$

4. $\dfrac{9}{20} \times \dfrac{8}{9} =$

5. $\dfrac{13}{14} \times \dfrac{7}{8} =$

6. $\dfrac{5}{6} \times \dfrac{3}{4} =$

7. $\dfrac{7}{8} \times \dfrac{5}{14} =$

8. $\dfrac{8}{9} \times \dfrac{27}{32} =$

9. $\dfrac{4}{17} \times \dfrac{17}{18} =$

10. $\dfrac{4}{7} \times \dfrac{5}{6} =$

11. $\dfrac{5}{8} \times \dfrac{8}{13} =$

12. $\dfrac{6}{7} \times \dfrac{4}{6} =$

13. $\dfrac{15}{16} \times \dfrac{32}{45} =$

14. $\dfrac{8}{14} \times \dfrac{7}{8} =$

15. $\dfrac{5}{6} \times \dfrac{6}{11} =$

16. $\dfrac{6}{13} \times \dfrac{9}{18} =$

17. $\dfrac{4}{27} \times \dfrac{1}{4} =$

18. $\dfrac{6}{28} \times \dfrac{7}{12} =$

19. $\dfrac{8}{20} \times \dfrac{20}{32} =$

20. $\dfrac{1}{16} \times \dfrac{8}{13} =$

21. $\dfrac{3}{15} \times \dfrac{5}{16} =$

22. $\dfrac{7}{24} \times \dfrac{8}{42} =$

23. $\dfrac{7}{50} \times \dfrac{25}{14} =$

24. $\dfrac{4}{27} \times \dfrac{9}{16} =$

Before you can multiply mixed numbers, you must change them to improper fractions. Then you multiply the numerators and the denominators.

Example: Find the product of $2\frac{2}{3}$ and $3\frac{1}{4}$.

Step 1: Write the mixed numbers as improper fractions.

$$2\frac{2}{3} \times 3\frac{1}{4} = \frac{8}{3} \times \frac{13}{4}$$

Step 2: Simplify if possible.

$$\frac{\overset{2}{\cancel{8}}}{3} \times \frac{13}{\underset{1}{\cancel{4}}}$$

Step 3: Multiply.

$$\frac{\overset{2}{\cancel{8}}}{3} \times \frac{13}{\underset{1}{\cancel{4}}} = \frac{26}{3} = 8\frac{2}{3}$$

A Change these mixed numbers to improper fractions.

1. $3\frac{3}{5}$

2. $4\frac{4}{6}$

3. $2\frac{11}{12}$

4. $11\frac{1}{5}$

5. $7\frac{9}{10}$

6. $2\frac{8}{12}$

7. $8\frac{2}{13}$

8. $1\frac{8}{9}$

9. $5\frac{10}{17}$

10. $3\frac{8}{9}$

B Multiply these fractions. Write your answers in lowest terms.

11. $1\frac{1}{3} \times 2\frac{1}{5} =$

12. $4\frac{3}{5} \times 1\frac{2}{3} =$

13. $3\frac{3}{5} \times 5\frac{7}{8} =$

14. $3\frac{1}{2} \times 2\frac{1}{2} =$

15. $1\frac{2}{3} \times \frac{1}{10} =$

16. $4\frac{2}{3} \times 1\frac{1}{7} =$

17. $1\frac{2}{7} \times 4\frac{2}{3} =$

18. $2\frac{3}{5} \times 10 =$

19. $4\frac{1}{3} \times \frac{3}{7} =$

20. $3\frac{1}{3} \times 2\frac{1}{5} =$

21. $5\frac{3}{7} \times \frac{2}{19} =$

22. $3\frac{2}{9} \times 1\frac{1}{5} =$

23. $2\frac{1}{4} \times 12 =$

24. $\frac{5}{18} \times 3\frac{3}{5} =$

25. $2\frac{2}{9} \times 3\frac{3}{5} =$

26. $1\frac{3}{5} \times 2\frac{4}{5} =$

27. $5\frac{1}{3} \times 1\frac{5}{7} =$

28. $6\frac{3}{4} \times 1\frac{10}{30} =$

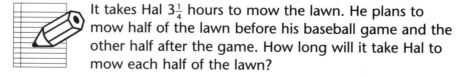

It takes Hal $3\frac{1}{4}$ hours to mow the lawn. He plans to mow half of the lawn before his baseball game and the other half after the game. How long will it take Hal to mow each half of the lawn?

_____

Dividing Fractions

The easiest way to divide fractions is to invert the divisor and then multiply.

Turning a fraction upside down is called *inverting*.

Divisor

Example: $\dfrac{4}{13} \div \dfrac{2}{5} = ?$

Step 1: Invert the divisor.

Step 2: Multiply. Write the answer in lowest terms.

$$\dfrac{4}{13} \div \dfrac{2}{5} = \dfrac{4}{13} \times \dfrac{5}{2}$$

$$\dfrac{4}{13} \times \dfrac{5}{2} = \dfrac{20}{26} = \dfrac{10}{13}$$

To divide by a fraction, invert the divisor and multiply.

Example: Find the quotient for $\dfrac{14}{15} \div \dfrac{7}{45}$

Step 1: Invert the divisor.

Step 2: Simplify if possible. Then multiply.

$$\dfrac{14}{15} \div \dfrac{7}{45} = \dfrac{\overset{2}{14}}{\underset{1}{15}} \times \dfrac{\overset{3}{45}}{\underset{1}{7}}$$

$$\dfrac{2}{1} \times \dfrac{3}{1} = \dfrac{6}{1} = 6$$

Divide. Write your answers in lowest terms.

1. $\dfrac{10}{12} \div \dfrac{6}{7} =$

2. $\dfrac{3}{10} \div \dfrac{6}{5} =$

3. $\dfrac{5}{6} \div \dfrac{10}{11} =$

4. $\dfrac{7}{8} \div \dfrac{13}{16} =$

5. $\dfrac{12}{14} \div \dfrac{3}{4} =$

6. $\dfrac{4}{5} \div \dfrac{6}{5} =$

7. $\dfrac{6}{7} \div \dfrac{8}{10} =$

8. $\dfrac{5}{9} \div \dfrac{15}{18} =$

9. $\dfrac{11}{12} \div \dfrac{10}{12} =$

10. $\dfrac{2}{15} \div \dfrac{4}{5} =$

11. $\dfrac{20}{21} \div \dfrac{10}{7} =$

12. $\dfrac{6}{10} \div \dfrac{26}{30} =$

13. $\dfrac{10}{17} \div \dfrac{15}{34} =$

14. $\dfrac{3}{11} \div \dfrac{7}{8} =$

15. $\dfrac{11}{20} \div \dfrac{33}{32} =$

16. $\dfrac{16}{12} \div \dfrac{36}{30} =$

17. $\dfrac{2}{11} \div \dfrac{11}{22} =$

18. $\dfrac{3}{14} \div \dfrac{1}{16} =$

19. $\dfrac{13}{20} \div \dfrac{13}{20} =$

20. $\dfrac{14}{19} \div \dfrac{16}{11} =$

Dividing Mixed Numbers

In order to divide mixed numbers, you first change the mixed numbers to improper fractions. Then you invert the divisor and multiply.

Example: Find the quotient for $2\frac{2}{3} \div \frac{5}{6}$.

Step 1: Express mixed numbers as improper fractions.

Step 2: Invert the divisor, simplify if possible, and multiply.

Step 3: Simplify the answer.

$$2\frac{2}{3} \div \frac{5}{6} = \frac{8}{3} \div \frac{5}{6}$$

$$\frac{8}{\underset{1}{\cancel{3}}} \times \frac{\cancel{6}^{2}}{5} = \frac{8}{1} \times \frac{2}{5} = \frac{16}{5}$$

$$\frac{16}{5} = 3\frac{1}{5}$$

Divide. Write your answers in lowest terms.

1. $1\frac{3}{6} \div \frac{12}{15} =$

2. $1\frac{5}{12} \div 2\frac{1}{6} =$

3. $\frac{8}{15} \div 2\frac{1}{2} =$

4. $3\frac{1}{8} \div 2\frac{3}{4} =$

5. $1\frac{3}{4} \div 1\frac{1}{8} =$

6. $16 \div 1\frac{1}{2} =$

7. $2\frac{4}{5} \div 2\frac{8}{10} =$

8. $6\frac{3}{7} \div 4\frac{1}{2} =$

9. $2\frac{3}{5} \div 6 =$

10. $1\frac{6}{7} \div \frac{7}{6} =$

11. $2\frac{8}{10} \div \frac{4}{5} =$

12. $\frac{5}{6} \div 1\frac{2}{3} =$

13. $2\frac{2}{3} \div 4 =$

14. $4\frac{1}{3} \div 2\frac{1}{3} =$

15. $2\frac{1}{5} \div 6 =$

16. $2\frac{1}{2} \div 1\frac{3}{6} =$

17. $1\frac{5}{9} \div 5\frac{1}{3} =$

18. $2\frac{2}{3} \div 3\frac{2}{9} =$

19. $5 \div 3\frac{3}{4} =$

20. $3\frac{3}{5} \div 9\frac{1}{3} =$

21. $6 \div 1\frac{4}{5} =$

 Claire has $22\frac{1}{2}$ yards of fabric. She wants to make holiday vests for her friends. Each vest requires $2\frac{1}{4}$ yards of fabric. How many vests can Claire make?

_____

Comparing Fractions

There is a special way to compare fractions by using mathematics. All you have to do is *cross-multiply*. This means that you multiply the numerator of one factor by the denominator of the other factor. Then you multiply the denominator of one factor by the numerator of the other factor.

Example: Compare $\frac{4}{9}$ and $\frac{1}{2}$.

$$\frac{4}{9} \qquad \frac{1}{2}$$

Step 1: Multiply one numerator by one denominator.

Step 2: Multiply the other numerator by the other denominator.

$$\overset{®}{\frac{4}{9}} \diagdown\diagup \overset{⑨}{\frac{1}{2}}$$

Step 3: Write the products near the numerator.

$$8 \quad < \quad 9$$

Step 4: The fractions have the same relationship as the products.

Therefore, $\frac{4}{9} \quad < \quad \frac{1}{2}$

◼ Write >, <, or = for each pair of fractions.

1. $\frac{5}{12}$ ◯ $\frac{4}{8}$

2. $\frac{3}{4}$ ◯ $\frac{6}{8}$

3. $\frac{9}{12}$ ◯ $\frac{5}{7}$

4. $\frac{4}{13}$ ◯ $\frac{3}{14}$

5. $\frac{7}{8}$ ◯ $\frac{5}{6}$

6. $\frac{2}{16}$ ◯ $\frac{3}{15}$

7. $\frac{8}{25}$ ◯ $\frac{4}{30}$

8. $\frac{5}{16}$ ◯ $\frac{4}{13}$

9. $\frac{11}{12}$ ◯ $\frac{12}{13}$

10. $\frac{7}{16}$ ◯ $\frac{5}{14}$

11. $\frac{5}{6}$ ◯ $\frac{5}{7}$

12. $\frac{3}{5}$ ◯ $\frac{5}{13}$

13. $\frac{18}{20}$ ◯ $\frac{9}{10}$

14. $\frac{9}{20}$ ◯ $\frac{4}{10}$

15. $\frac{5}{30}$ ◯ $\frac{6}{30}$

16. $\frac{13}{26}$ ◯ $\frac{10}{20}$

17. $\frac{5}{12}$ ◯ $\frac{6}{13}$

18. $\frac{11}{15}$ ◯ $\frac{12}{16}$

19. $\frac{6}{17}$ ◯ $\frac{12}{34}$

20. $\frac{8}{19}$ ◯ $\frac{16}{31}$

21. $\frac{12}{13}$ ◯ $\frac{13}{14}$

22. $\frac{3}{11}$ ◯ $\frac{4}{12}$

23. $\frac{8}{16}$ ◯ $\frac{5}{15}$

24. $\frac{11}{22}$ ◯ $\frac{22}{55}$

Solve these problems. Express your answers in lowest terms.

1. Mateo brought $21\frac{1}{2}$ pounds of aluminum cans and $4\frac{1}{6}$ pounds of copper wire to the recycling center. How many pounds of metal did Mateo recycle?

    _____

2. Gail filled up her gas tank on Tuesday. On Wednesday, she used $\frac{1}{8}$ tank of gas. On Thursday, she used $\frac{1}{2}$ tank. How much gas did Gail have left?

    _____

3. The Alpine Runners ran $16\frac{1}{3}$ miles in 4 hours. How many miles did they run in one hour?

    _____

4. Ki spent $3\frac{1}{4}$ hours each day building a deck. He worked for 7 days. How many hours did it take Ki to build his deck?

    _____

5. There are 640 students at Ridge School. Of these, $\frac{1}{8}$ ride the bus to school. How many students ride the bus?

    _____

6. A crate of apples weighs 18 pounds. The crate itself weighs $1\frac{3}{7}$ pounds. How much do the apples weigh?

    _____

7. Penny brought 42 bushels of tomatoes to sell at the farmers' market. She sold $1\frac{1}{2}$ bushels, $3\frac{1}{6}$ bushels, 9 bushels, $5\frac{3}{12}$ bushels, and $4\frac{3}{4}$ bushels. How many bushels of tomatoes were left at the end of the day?

    _____

8. Xavier earns $6.00 per hour at his part-time job at the bookstore. If he works on the weekend, he earns $1\frac{1}{2}$ times his base pay. What is Xavier's weekend pay rate?

    _____

9. A landscape crew of 7 people was assigned to seed a $3\frac{1}{4}$-acre field. How much of the field will each crew member seed?

    _____

10. Yao has invited 20 friends to a party. He made 4 submarine sandwiches and cut each sandwich into fourths. Does Yao have enough sandwiches to serve each of his friends?

    _____

Proficiency Test 2

Circle the correct answer.

1. $\frac{4}{5} \times 3\frac{1}{3} =$

    a. $3\frac{4}{15}$

    b. $3\frac{5}{8}$

    c. 8

    d. $2\frac{2}{3}$

2. $\frac{1}{4} + 5\frac{1}{6} =$

    a. $5\frac{11}{12}$

    b. $5\frac{3}{5}$

    c. $5\frac{12}{13}$

    d. $5\frac{5}{12}$

3. $\frac{11}{12} - \frac{2}{3} =$

    a. $\frac{1}{4}$

    b. $\frac{7}{12}$

    c. 1

    d. $\frac{4}{9}$

4. $3\frac{1}{2} \div 4\frac{1}{2} =$

    a. $1\frac{2}{9}$

    b. $\frac{7}{9}$

    c. $1\frac{2}{7}$

    d. $\frac{9}{7}$

5. $\frac{7}{12}$ expressed in higher terms is

    a. $\frac{14}{19}$

    b. $\frac{70}{100}$

    c. $\frac{28}{48}$

    d. $\frac{7}{48}$

6. $5\frac{4}{9}$ expressed as an improper fraction is

    a. $\frac{45}{9}$

    b. $\frac{49}{9}$

    c. $\frac{45}{49}$

    d. $\frac{20}{9}$

7. $5\frac{3}{8}$

   $+ 11\frac{1}{8}$

    a. $16\frac{1}{2}$

    b. $11\frac{1}{2}$

    c. $16\frac{3}{8}$

    d. 16

8. $\frac{54}{10}$ renamed as a mixed number =

    a. $5\frac{1}{2}$

    b. $10\frac{4}{10}$

    c. 54

    d. $5\frac{2}{5}$

9. $\frac{14}{15} - \frac{9}{15} =$

    a. $\frac{1}{5}$

    b. $\frac{6}{15}$

    c. $\frac{1}{3}$

    d. $\frac{1}{4}$

10. $\frac{8}{48}$ reduced to its lowest terms =

    a. $\frac{1}{6}$

    b. $\frac{1}{8}$

    c. $\frac{1}{4}$

    d. $\frac{1}{7}$

11. $20\frac{11}{9}$ renamed is

    a. $21\frac{2}{9}$

    b. $21\frac{1}{9}$

    c. 22

    d. $20\frac{9}{11}$

12. $5\frac{1}{3} \times 2\frac{3}{4} =$

    a. 10

    b. $10\frac{3}{12}$

    c. $14\frac{2}{3}$

    d. $14\frac{1}{2}$

13. The least common multiple of 4 and 3 is

    a. 6

    b. 8

    c. 24

    d. 12

14. $30\frac{1}{2} - 15\frac{1}{4} =$

    a. 15

    b. $14\frac{3}{4}$

    c. $15\frac{1}{4}$

    d. $15\frac{1}{2}$

15.   20

   $- 13\frac{4}{9}$

    a. $5\frac{4}{9}$

    b. $6\frac{5}{9}$

    c. 6

    d. $5\frac{5}{9}$

16. $5\frac{4}{5} \div 1\frac{1}{2} =$

    a. $7\frac{1}{2}$

    b. $3\frac{13}{15}$

    c. $8\frac{7}{10}$

    d. $3\frac{2}{3}$

17. $\frac{1}{3} \times \frac{1}{3} =$

    a. $\frac{2}{3}$

    b. $\frac{1}{6}$

    c. $\frac{1}{9}$

    d. 1

18. Which fraction is <u>not</u> equal to $\frac{3}{4}$?

    a. $\frac{11}{33}$

    b. $\frac{75}{100}$

    c. $\frac{6}{8}$

    d. $\frac{21}{28}$

19. $\frac{12}{132}$ reduces to

    a. $\frac{6}{66}$

    b. $\frac{6}{12}$

    c. $\frac{3}{33}$

    d. $\frac{1}{11}$

20. $10\frac{3}{10}$ expressed as an improper fraction is

    a. $\frac{30}{10}$

    b. $\frac{23}{10}$

    c. $\frac{103}{10}$

    d. $\frac{33}{10}$

Introducing Decimals

U N I T 4

Reading decimals and writing decimals both require the use of a four-step method.

Step 1: Read the whole-number portion.

Step 2: Say *and* for the decimal point.

Step 3: Read the digits to the right of the decimal point as if they were a whole number.

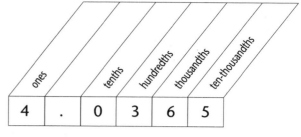

Step 4: Finish by saying the place name of the last digit.

Example: Read the decimal numeral 4.0365.

    1. four ——————► **4.0365** ◄—————— 4. ten-thousandths

         2. and ╱   3. three hundred sixty-five

four and three hundred sixty-five ten-thousandths

Example: Read the decimal number 0.23.
(This number may also be written as .23.)
Skip steps one and two if there is no whole-number portion.
The decimal number 0.23 is read and written as **twenty-three hundredths.**

Write the word names for these decimal numbers.

1. 2.605 _____

2. 14.07 _____

3. 0.1723 _____

4. .1 _____

5. 14.2 _____

6. 1.6 _____

7. 17.003 _____

8. 1.77 _____

9. 29.1 _____

10. 0.22 _____

11. .22 _____

12. 0.01 _____

Translating Written Decimals

If you have to change word decimals back into number form, it's very important to remember the place values those decimals have. Since there is no way to say *zero* when you read or write decimals, the only way you can let others know it is there is by indicating the place value of the last digit.

Example:	Write the decimal numeral for the word name "seven and two hundred fifty-six ten-thousandths."	
Step 1:	Write the numbers as you hear them.	7.256
Step 2:	Count the places in your number. Is the last place name the same as in the word form?	No, 6 is in the thousandths place.
Step 3:	Insert zeros to put numbers in correct place value. Place the zeros to the right of the decimal point. Now, 6 is the ten-thousandths place.	7.0256

Other Examples: Nine and eight hundredths = 9.08
Sixty-three ten-thousandths = 0.0063 or .0063

■ Write the decimal numerals for these word names.

1. six and twenty-four hundredths _____

2. sixteen and sixteen thousandths _____

3. twelve hundredths _____

4. five hundred and nine hundredths _____

5. two hundred and three ten-thousandths _____

6. fifty-six and four hundred eleven ten-thousandths _____

7. three hundred forty-one hundred-thousandths _____

8. sixty and twelve hundred-thousandths _____

9. nine thousandths _____

10. seven thousand forty-five ten-thousandths _____

11. thirteen hundredths _____

12. fifteen and eighteen hundred-thousandths _____

13. nine and eight hundred-thousandths _____

14. nine and eight ten-thousandths _____

15. fifty-two hundredths _____

16. seventy-five thousandths _____

Comparing Decimals

It is easy to compare decimals just by lining them up vertically.

Example: Compare 0.063 and 0.0198, using <, >, or =.

Step 1: Write one number over the other with the decimal points in a vertical line. $\quad$ 0.063
0.0198

Step 2: Insert zeros in the spaces. $\quad$ 0.063**0**
0.0198

Step 3: Ignore the decimal points and the zeros on the left. $\quad$ 630

Step 4: Since 198 < 630, 0.0198 < 0.063 $\quad$ 198

If there is a whole number before the decimal, it must be considered first, before you work with the decimals.

Example: 2.1 > 1.985, because 2 > 1.

Note: The symbols > and < will always point to the smaller number.

A Use one of these symbols, < or >, for each pair of numbers.

1. 1.06 ◯ 1.007

2. 5.17 ◯ 2.298

3. 0.8 ◯ 0.19

4. 3.1 ◯ 0.325

5. 5.0 ◯ 0.51

6. 4.12 ◯ 4.034

7. 5.015 ◯ .1006

8. 2.54 ◯ .225

9. 5.012 ◯ 5.120

10. 106.2 ◯ 50.7

11. 1010.11 ◯ 1.111

12. 0.0234 ◯ 0.222

13. 7.1 ◯ .85

14. .340 ◯ 1.67

15. 92.341 ◯ 92.049

B Arrange these decimals from greatest to least.

16. 0.162, 0.1073, 1.7

17. 5.551, 5.6, 4.823

18. 0.704, 7.03, 0.0703

19. 1.7, 17, .701

20. 0.51, 1.5, 0.502

21. 0.8018, 0.8081, .808

22. 0.6602, .7714, .67

23. 8.8, 8.088, 8

Decimals and Fractions

The decimal 0.5 and the fraction $\frac{1}{2}$ name the same number. Decimals and fractions are both names for parts of a whole.

$$\frac{1}{2} = \frac{1}{2} \times \frac{5}{5} = \frac{5}{10} = 0.5$$

You can find the decimal equivalent by finding an equivalent common fraction with a denominator of 10, 100, 1000.

Example: $\frac{1}{4} = \frac{25}{100} = 0.25$

A Find the decimal equivalent for these fractions.

1. $\frac{3}{5}$ 2. $\frac{1}{8}$ 3. $\frac{3}{4}$ 4. $\frac{7}{8}$ 5. $\frac{7}{10}$

You can also find the decimal equivalent by dividing the fraction.

Example: $\frac{3}{8} =$

$$
\begin{array}{r}
.375 \\
8\overline{)3.000} \\
\underline{24} \\
60 \\
\underline{56} \\
40 \\
\underline{40} \\
0
\end{array}
$$

B Use the division method to find the decimal equivalents.

6. $\frac{1}{2}$ 7. $\frac{13}{20}$ 8. $\frac{5}{8}$ 9. $\frac{1}{4}$ 10. $\frac{1}{5}$

Use a calculator to solve this problem. Teresa earns $26,240 per year. Last year, she worked $\frac{5}{8}$ of the year. How much did Teresa earn last year?

Think: $\frac{5}{8} \times \frac{26,240}{1}$

_____

UNIT 4

The procedure for rounding decimals is just like rounding whole numbers. The first steps are the same: to identify the place names.

Example: Round 4.467 to the nearest tenth.

Step 1:   Identify the place of rounding.   4.<u>4</u>67 **tenths place**

Step 2:   If the digit to the right is 5 or more, add 1 to the place of   4.<u>4</u>67
                rounding.

Step 3:   Drop all digits to the right of the place of rounding.   4.5

Example: Round 3.7849 to the nearest hundredth.   3.7<u>8</u>49 **hundredths place**

Step 1:   Identify the place of rounding.
                                                                                                        3.7<u>8</u>49
Step 2:   If the digit to the right is less than 5, then do not add 1.

Step 3:   Drop all digits to the right of the place of rounding.   3.78

Complete this chart by rounding each number to the place indicated.

Tenths	Hundredths	Thousandths
1. 4.62 _____	9. 5.017 _____	17. 0.0925 _____
2. 6.27 _____	10. 3.785 _____	18. 0.6291 _____
3. 0.79 _____	11. 0.4115 _____	19. 0.1288 _____
4. 0.96 _____	12. 1.063 _____	20. 9.00336 _____
5. 0.059 _____	13. 0.3098 _____	21. 5.16823 _____
6. 96.01 _____	14. 0.1951 _____	22. 28.41231 _____
7. 0.049 _____	15. 2.1191 _____	23. 0.62483 _____
8. 126.19 _____	16. 285.092 _____	24. 0.00781 _____

Adding Decimals

When you add decimals, you follow the rules for adding whole numbers. You also have to take the extra step of making sure the decimal points are lined up vertically. You do this to make sure you add tenths to tenths, hundredths to hundredths, and so on.

Example: Find the sum of 2.83, 5, and 9.1.

Step 1: Write the decimal numerals in a vertical format with the decimal points in a vertical line.

$$\begin{array}{r} 2.83 \\ 5. \\ 9.1 \end{array}$$

Remember: Every whole number has a a decimal point.

Step 2: Write zeros in all of the blank spaces, if you want, to help avoid confusion.

$$\begin{array}{r} 2.83 \\ 5.00 \\ + 9.10 \end{array}$$

Step 3: Add.

$$\begin{array}{r} 2.83 \\ 5.00 \\ + 9.10 \\ \hline 16.93 \end{array}$$

A Find the sums.

1. $\begin{array}{r} 2.8 \\ + 3.56 \end{array}$

2. $\begin{array}{r} 8 \\ 9.2 \\ + 0.5 \end{array}$

3. $\begin{array}{r} 1.26 \\ 0.83 \\ + 0.6 \end{array}$

4. $\begin{array}{r} 123.081 \\ 20.16 \\ + \quad 5 \end{array}$

B Write these addends vertically and add.

5. $12.3 + 8.4 + 7$

6. $4.9 + 6 + 1.45$

7. $9 + 1.4 + 0.41$

8. $14.8 + 2.3 + 6$

9. $3 + 8.05 + 1.7$

10. $18 + 6.2 + 3.11$

11. $8.1 + 7 + 1.21$

12. $8 + 2.1 + 4.021$

13. $5 + 2.35 + 0.15$

Use the addition key on a calculator to find the sum. Hidori walked 5 km to the store. Then she walked 1.492 km to the library and .54 km to the park. How many kilometers did Hidori walk?

_____

Subtracting Decimals

Subtracting decimals is just like subtracting whole numbers. You follow the same rules. Just as in addition, you have to make sure the decimal points are lined up vertically.

Note: When you subtract, write the "From" term on the top line.
Write the "Subtract" term on the second line. Then subtract.

Example: From 16.2 subtract 1.83.

This means the same as 16.2 – 1.83.

Step 1:   Write the **from** term number first.

$$16.2$$

Step 2:   Write the number to be subtracted below the first number. Then insert **zeros** in the spaces and subtract.

$$\begin{array}{r} 16.20 \\ -\ 1.83 \\ \hline 14.37 \end{array}$$

Write these subtraction problems in vertical form and subtract.

1. 18 – 16.25 =

2. 21.7 – 18.39 =

3. 35 – 4.8 =

4. 6 – 2.14 =

5. 5.5 – 1.73 =

6. 12.85 – 1.6 =

7. 18.4 – 1.3 =

8. 26.4 – 0.45 =

9. 5.4 – 0.96 =

10. 2 – 0.091 =

11. 3 – 0.048 =

12. 10 – 3.72 =

13. 35 – 0.0621 =

14. 12 – 8.1 =

15. 11 – 10.3 =

Multiplying Decimals

When you multiply decimals, you follow the same rules that you use to multiply whole numbers.

There is a simple rule to follow to find out where to insert the decimal point in your answers. Count the decimal places in each factor. Add them up. In the products, start at the right and count over that number of decimal places. Write your decimal point there.

Examples:

Find the product of 3.17 and 21.5.

```
    3.17   2 places ┐
  x 21.5   1 place  ├──► 3 places
    1585             ┘
    317
    634
  68.155   3 places
```

Find the product of 41.1 and 0.213.

```
    41.1   1 place  ┐
  x .213   3 places ├──► 4 places
    1233             ┘
    411
    822
  8.7543   4 places
```

◼ Find the product of these decimals.

1. 2.1 x 4.3	2. 3.6 x .41	3. 6.1 x 1.2	4. 8.9 x 2.1	5. 6.2 x .85	6. .81 x .95
7. 5.19 x 4.3	8. 3.62 x 1.5	9. 11.5 x 4.6	10. 31.4 x 6.3	11. 8.21 x .21	12. 9.12 x 6.3
13. 4.23 x 1.03	14. 51.2 x 2.06	15. 30.1 x 2.05	16. 6.15 x 30.3	17. 1.18 x 2.09	18. 8.11 x 1.01

The Booster Club sold 90 boxes of oranges, 32 boxes of apples, and 41 boxes of grapefruit to raise money for new band uniforms. The Boosters charged $4.50 a box for oranges, $3.00 a box for apples, and $5.00 a box for grapefruit. How much did the Booster Club earn from the fruit sales? _____

Adding Zeros When You Multiply

After you have done the multiplication in some problems, you may find that there are not enough place values to put the decimal point in the answer. Therefore, you add zeros to the left of the product.

Example: Find the product of 0.24 and 0.06.

Step 1: Find the product as shown.

```
        .24    2 places ┐
      x .06    2 places ┘──► 4 places
        144    need 4 places
```

Step 2: Write zeros to the left of the product to make the total number of places needed.

$0.24 \times 0.06 = .0144$

Examples:

```
   2.34    2 places              .24    2 places
 x .002   +3 places            x .1    +1 place
 .00468    5 places            .024    3 places
```

A Multiply. Write the decimal points in the proper place.

1. .46	2. 3.19	3. .56	4. .069	5. .623
x .05	x .02	x .09	x .018	x.005

6. .923	7. 7.85	8. 2.19	9. .615	10. .005
x .03	x .003	x .04	x .009	x .005

B Find the products.

11. .251	12. .351	13. 1.09	14. .029	15. .118
x .05	x .08	x .001	x .024	x .01

16. .412	17. 1.45	18. .023	19. .006	20. .141
x .06	x .009	x .025	x .011	x .07

Dividing Decimals by Whole Numbers

Lesson 10

Division of decimals by whole numbers can be expressed in three different ways. Look at the example.

Example: Divide 16.8 by 8. This means the same as

$$16.8 \div 8 \quad \text{or} \quad \frac{16.8}{8} \quad \text{or} \quad 8\overline{)16.8}$$

Step 1:   Notice that the divisor is a whole number.

$$8\overline{)16.8}$$

Step 2:   Find the decimal point in the dividend. Write a new decimal point directly above it.

$$8\overline{)16.8}$$

Step 3:   Divide. Use the same rules you follow when you divide.

$$\begin{array}{r} 2.1 \\ 8\overline{)16.8} \\ \underline{16} \\ 8 \\ \underline{8} \end{array}$$

Find the quotients for these division problems. Each quotient will end on or before the thousandths place.

1. $6\overline{)11.4}$

2. $7\overline{)17.5}$

3. $16\overline{)28.8}$

4. $28\overline{)70.28}$

5. $36\overline{)111.6}$

6. $5\overline{)1.15}$

7. $11\overline{)44.11}$

8. $9\overline{)49.95}$

9. $6\overline{)5.58}$

10. $13\overline{)33.8}$

11. $14\overline{)58.8}$

12. $3\overline{)3.09}$

13. $15\overline{)9.3}$

14. $45\overline{)45.45}$

15. $9\overline{)23.67}$

16. $28\overline{)3.08}$

17. $11\overline{)2.541}$

18. $9\overline{).315}$

19. $3\overline{).267}$

20. $12\overline{)1.344}$

Carla needs to buy tickets for her club for an upcoming soccer game. She has $144.00. How many $32 tickets can she buy?

_____

UNIT 4

Dividing by a decimal follows the same general rules of dividing with whole numbers. However, you must be careful when you place a decimal point in the quotient. Follow these steps.

divisor

Example: Divide 4.96 by 0.8.

$0.8\overline{)4.96}$ ← dividend

Step 1: Move the decimal point in the divisor to the right.

$.8\overline{)4.96}$

Step 2: Move the decimal point in the dividend to the right the same number of places.

$$
\begin{array}{r}
6.2 \\
8\overline{)49.6} \\
\underline{48} \\
16 \\
\underline{16}
\end{array}
$$

← quotient

Step 3: Divide. Place a decimal point in quotient directly above the new place in the dividend.

■ Find the quotients for these division problems. Each quotient will end on or before the thousandths place.

1. $.9\overline{)1.296}$

2. $.4\overline{).68}$

3. $.8\overline{)2.08}$

4. $.5\overline{)1.85}$

5. $3.2\overline{)9.28}$

6. $.6\overline{).624}$

7. $1.3\overline{).0325}$

8. $2.8\overline{).476}$

9. $3.3\overline{)16.83}$

10. $2.1\overline{).0714}$

11. $.8\overline{).0368}$

12. $.9\overline{).1215}$

13. $.06\overline{).0858}$

14. $3.8\overline{)80.94}$

15. $5.6\overline{)107.52}$

16. $1.1\overline{)4.95}$

17. $1.8\overline{)4.14}$

18. $5.8\overline{)29.58}$

19. $2.1\overline{).0042}$

20. $1.5\overline{).0195}$

Zeros in the Dividend

Sometimes, you have to add zeros to the dividend in order to provide enough places to move the decimal point.

Example: Divide 3.6 by .12.

Step 1:

$.12\overline{)3.6}$

Move decimal point in divisor 2 places.

Step 2:

$12\overline{)360.}$

Move decimal point in dividend 2 places; fill in with a zero.

Step 3:

$$\begin{array}{r} 30. \\ 12\overline{)360.} \\ \underline{36} \\ 00 \end{array}$$

Divide and place decimal point in quotient.

Divide. Each quotient will end on or before the thousandths place.

1. $.03\overline{)9}$

2. $.02\overline{)8}$

3. $.04\overline{)8.4}$

4. $.09\overline{)8.1}$

5. $.06\overline{)7.2}$

6. $.02\overline{)12.8}$

7. $.04\overline{)84.8}$

8. $.03\overline{)12.9}$

9. $.05\overline{)25.5}$

10. $.07\overline{)56.7}$

11. $.09\overline{)81.9}$

12. $.02\overline{)24.6}$

13. $.05\overline{)86.5}$

14. $.06\overline{)13.2}$

15. $.07\overline{)24.5}$

16. $.07\overline{)85.4}$

17. $.13\overline{)27.3}$

18. $.12\overline{)27.6}$

19. $.15\overline{)49.5}$

20. $.11\overline{)23.1}$

21. $.31\overline{)99.2}$

22. $.32\overline{)67.2}$

23. $.06\overline{)97.2}$

24. $.63\overline{)151.2}$

Powers of Ten

Multiplying or dividing by 10 is simple. You can do it just by moving the decimal point. Even if you are working with powers of 10 (hundreds, thousands, ten thousands, etc.), the same rule can still be used.

When you find a zero in the multiplier, you can move the decimal point in the multiplicand to find the answer. Move the decimal point to the right. When you find a zero in the divisor, you can move the decimal point in the divisor to find the answer. Move the decimal point to the left.

Examples:

24.8	x	10	=	248.0
2.48	x	100	=	248.00
.248	x	1000	=	248.000
multiplicand		**multiplier**		

Rules:
Count the zeros in the multiplier. Move the decimal point in the multiplicand one place to the right for each zero to find the answer.

348000.	÷	100	=	3480
34800.	÷	10	=	3480
dividend		**divisor**		

Rules:
Count the zeros in the divisor. Move the decimal point in the dividend one place to the left for each zero to find the answer.

A Multiply by these powers of 10.

1. 263 x 10 = _____

2. 829 x 100 = _____

3. 39 x 1,000 = _____

4. 6,213 x 100 = _____

5. 4,120 x 10 = _____

6. 26.5 x 100 = _____

7. 232 x 100 = _____

8. 20 x 100 = _____

9. 9,111 x 10 = _____

10. 401 x 10 = _____

B Divide by these powers of 10.

11. 3,800 ÷ 10 = _____

12. 680 ÷ 10 = _____

13. 2,900 ÷ 100 = _____

14. 79,000 ÷ 10 = _____

15. 12,000 ÷ 10 = _____

16. 30,000 ÷ 10 = _____

17. 54,000 ÷ 1,000 = _____

18. 390 ÷ 10 = _____

19. 234,000,000 ÷ 100,000 = _____

20. 100,000 ÷ 1,000 = _____

Proficiency Test 3

  Circle the correct answer.

1. 3.64 + 8 + 2.7 =
   a. 7.14
   b. 3.99
   c. 14.34
   d. 6.42

2. 18 − .38 =
   a. 17.62
   b. 18.38
   c. .20
   d. 17.38

3. .36 x .004 =
   a. .144
   b. .0144
   c. .00144
   d. 1.44

4. The numeral for twenty hundredths is
   a. 20.0
   b. .20
   c. .020
   d. .002

5. 12.629 rounded to the nearest tenth is
   a. 12.63
   b. 12.61
   c. 12.7
   d. 12.6

6.   111.1
        15.6
     + 5.0
   a. 131.7
   b. 127.2
   c. 626.7
   d. 1272

7. Which digit is in the thousandths place in the number 9.1274?
   a. 1
   b. 2
   c. 7
   d. 4

8. Which number has the greatest value?
   a. 1.7
   b. 11.7
   c. .117
   d. 11.77

9. 174.23 − 18.9 =
   a. 174.04
   b. 155.33
   c. 17.23
   d. 172.34

10. 2.6 x .73 =
   a. 1898
   b. 18.98
   c. 1.898
   d. .1898

11. 14)3.934 =
   a. .281
   b. 2.81
   c. 28.1
   d. 281

12. 87.000 ÷ 100 =
   a. 8.7
   b. 870
   c. .87
   d. 87

13.   .053
     x .005
   a. 2650
   b. 2.650
   c. .000265
   d. .0265

14. The numeral for five and three ten-thousandths is
   a. 5,003
   b. 5.030
   c. 5.0003
   d. 5.3

15. Which number is less than 7.07?
   a. 7.10
   b. 70.7
   c. .70
   d. 7.77

16. 4.02 x 2.04 =
   a. 82.08
   b. 8.2008
   c. 820.8
   d. 8,208

17. 2)52.24
   a. 261.2
   b. 26.12
   c. 2.612
   d. .2612

18. 7415 x 1000 =
   a. 741,500
   b. 7.415
   c. 74,150
   d. 7,415,000

19. .004)8.44 =
   a. 2.110
   b. 21.10
   c. 2110
   d. .211

20. $1.01 + $10.01 + .10 =
   a. $1.12
   b. $11.12
   c. $111.20
   d. $10.90

Writing Ratios

A *ratio* is a method of comparison using fractions. During one week (7 days), it was rainy 5 days and sunny 2 days. The ratio of rainy days to sunny days is 5 to 2. Ratios can also be expressed in other ways.

Example: The ratio of 4 circles to 3 squares can be written as

$$4 \text{ to } 3 \quad \text{ or } \quad \frac{4}{3} \quad \text{ or } \quad 4:3$$

The fractional form, $\frac{4}{3}$, is the most popular form because mathematical operations can be worked with ease.

Step 1:   Write the number of the first term as the numerator in the fraction.

Step 2:   Write the number of the second term as the denominator in the fraction.

Step 3:   Write the fraction in its lowest terms.

There are three squares, three shaded circles, four unshaded circles, and six triangles in the picture.

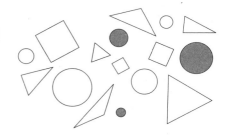

 Write a ratio to make each comparison. Use the fractional form. Express in lowest terms, if possible.

1. unshaded circles to triangles _____

2. squares to unshaded circles _____

3. triangles to unshaded circles _____

4. triangles to squares _____

5. unshaded circles to squares _____

6. squares to triangles _____

7. unshaded circles to all circles _____

8. all circles to triangles _____

9. squares to shaded circles _____

10. all circles to squares _____

Comparing Quantities

A Write a ratio to make each comparison. Use the fractional form. Write the ratio in lowest terms.

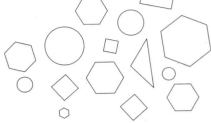

1. circles to hexagons _____
2. squares to hexagons _____
3. triangles to circles _____
4. hexagons to triangles _____
5. squares to circles _____
6. squares to triangles _____
7. hexagons to circles _____
8. circles to squares _____
9. triangles to hexagons _____
10. hexagons to squares _____
11. circles to triangles _____
12. triangles to squares _____

B Write a ratio to make each comparison. Use the fractional form. Write the ratio in lowest terms.

13. shaded circles to unshaded circles _____
14. unshaded rectangles to shaded triangles _____
15. unshaded triangles to shaded triangles _____
16. shaded triangles to all triangles _____
17. all rectangles to shaded circles _____
18. all circles to unshaded triangles _____
19. shaded circles to shaded triangles _____
20. shaded triangles to shaded circles _____
21. unshaded circles to shaded circles _____
22. all triangles to all circles _____

There are 3 teachers for every 12 students at Jefferson School. What is the ratio of students to teachers?

a. $\frac{1}{4}$ b. $\frac{4}{1}$ c. $\frac{1}{12}$ d. $\frac{12}{3}$

_____

Equal Ratios

Some ratios can be written in lower terms.
The ratio 12:16 can be expressed as 3:4.

Example: Use a ratio to make the following comparisons. Write the answer in lowest terms.

a.   6 pounds to $2.40 $\frac{6}{240}$ or $\frac{1}{40}$

b. to $\frac{15}{10}$ or $\frac{3}{2}$

c.   20 minutes to one hour $\frac{20}{60}$ or $\frac{1}{3}$

Write a ratio to make each comparison. Use the fractional form. Write the ratio in lowest terms.

1.  to _____

2. 45 minutes to 3 hours _____

3. 240 miles to 9 gallons _____

4. 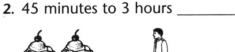 to  _____

5.  to _____

6. to _____

7. 8 dogs for 6 doghouses _____

8. 8 lamps for 20 desks _____

9. 12 ties for 3 shirts _____

10. 160 tires to 4 pumps _____

11. 6 hits for 8 times at bat _____

12. 10 crates for 56 books _____

13. 3 cars for 12 drivers _____

14. 480 apples for 10 pies _____

 Ernie made 9 free throws out of 12 attempts. What is Ernie's ratio of free throws to attempts?

_____

Comparing Ratios

You can easily find out whether two ratios are equal. To do this, you have to construct a proportion. A *proportion* has two parts: the means and the extremes.

$$\frac{2}{3} = \frac{4}{6} \text{ and } \overset{\text{means}}{2:3 = 4:6}$$

extremes

If the product of the means equals the product of the extremes, then the ratios are equal. In the above example, $3 \times 4 = 12$ and $2 \times 6 = 12$. Therefore, these two ratios are equal and form a proportion.

Examples:

$\frac{12}{15}$? $\frac{20}{25}$

20×15 ? 12×25

300 ? 300

$300 = 300$

$\frac{12}{15} = \frac{20}{25}$

$\frac{8}{12}$? $\frac{20}{25}$

20×12 ? 8×25

240 ? 200

$240 \neq 200$

$\frac{8}{12} \neq \frac{20}{25}$

The symbol for "is equal to" is =.　　**The symbol for "is not equal to" is ≠.**

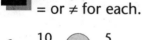 Multiply the means and extremes to tell which are proportions. Write = or ≠ for each.

1. $\frac{10}{16}$ ◯ $\frac{5}{8}$　　2. $\frac{12}{8}$ ◯ $\frac{9}{6}$　　3. $\frac{8}{6}$ ◯ $\frac{4}{3}$　　4. $\frac{20}{15}$ ◯ $\frac{7}{5}$

5. $\frac{15}{18}$ ◯ $\frac{2}{3}$　　6. $\frac{24}{6}$ ◯ $\frac{12}{3}$　　7. $\frac{10}{7}$ ◯ $\frac{12}{8}$　　8. $\frac{10}{12}$ ◯ $\frac{15}{18}$

9. $\frac{5}{6}$ ◯ $\frac{8}{9}$　　10. $\frac{4}{5}$ ◯ $\frac{3}{4}$　　11. $\frac{5}{9}$ ◯ $\frac{15}{27}$　　12. $\frac{9}{10}$ ◯ $\frac{11}{12}$

13. $\frac{4}{9}$ ◯ $\frac{6}{11}$　　14. $\frac{20}{21}$ ◯ $\frac{12}{14}$　　15. $\frac{10}{15}$ ◯ $\frac{33}{51}$　　16. $\frac{30}{10}$ ◯ $\frac{33}{11}$

Solving Proportions Using Cross Products

Suppose you are trying to find the missing number in a proportion. You can use the cross product method. When you use this method, you multiply the top of one ratio times the bottom of the other ratio. Then you multiply the bottom half of the first ratio times the top half of the second ratio.

Example:

$\frac{10}{N} = \frac{15}{30}$

$15 \times N = 10 \times 30$

$15 \times N = 300$

Step 1: Multiply on the diagonals.

$\frac{N}{12} = \frac{20}{24}$

$12 \times 20 = N \times 24$

Step 2: Simplify. In this case, you want to isolate the N from all other numbers. Since the problems call for you to multiply something times N, use the opposite operation—that is, division.

$240 = N \times 24$

$$\frac{15 \times N}{15} = \frac{300}{15}$$

$$\frac{^1\cancel{15} \times N}{\cancel{15}_1} = \frac{300}{15}$$

$$N = \frac{300}{15} = 20$$

$$\frac{10}{20} = \frac{15}{30}$$

Step 3: Complete with a final division.

$$\frac{240}{24} = \frac{N \times 24}{24}$$

$$\frac{240}{24} = \frac{N \times \cancel{24}^1}{\cancel{24}_1}$$

$$\frac{240}{24} = N$$

$$10 = N$$

Use the cross product method to solve for the missing number.

1. $\frac{3}{4} = \frac{N}{8}$

   N = _____

2. $\frac{5}{8} = \frac{6}{N}$

   N = _____

3. $\frac{4}{N} = \frac{1}{30}$

   N = _____

4. $\frac{5}{12} = \frac{4}{N}$

   N = _____

5. $\frac{4}{N} = \frac{12}{15}$

   N = _____

6. $\frac{5}{N} = \frac{6}{15}$

   N = _____

 It is 230 miles from Rochester to Duluth. If Barbara drives an average of 50 miles per hour, how long will it take her to make the trip?

_____

Using the Cross Product Method

 Use the cross product method to solve for the missing number.

1. $\dfrac{N}{6} = \dfrac{6}{9}$

   N = _____

2. $\dfrac{8}{12} = \dfrac{6}{N}$

   N = _____

3. $\dfrac{3}{8} = \dfrac{N}{32}$

   N = _____

4. $\dfrac{4}{N} = \dfrac{6}{15}$

   N = _____

5. $\dfrac{1}{3} = \dfrac{N}{6}$

   N = _____

6. $\dfrac{8}{25} = \dfrac{N}{10}$

   N = _____

7. $\dfrac{4}{12} = \dfrac{15}{N}$

   N = _____

8. $\dfrac{12}{N} = \dfrac{4}{9}$

   N = _____

9. $\dfrac{8}{3} = \dfrac{12}{N}$

   N = _____

10. $\dfrac{6}{10} = \dfrac{N}{8}$

    N = _____

11. $\dfrac{12}{8} = \dfrac{N}{5}$

    N = _____

12. $\dfrac{5}{8} = \dfrac{N}{12}$

    N = _____

13. $\dfrac{4}{5} = \dfrac{N}{60}$

    N = _____

14. $\dfrac{10}{13} = \dfrac{150}{N}$

    N = _____

15. $\dfrac{13}{N} = \dfrac{52}{20}$

    N = _____

16. $\dfrac{13}{15} = \dfrac{N}{45}$

    N = _____

17. $\dfrac{10}{24} = \dfrac{50}{N}$

    N = _____

18. $\dfrac{23}{N} = \dfrac{92}{28}$

    N = _____

19. $\dfrac{5}{N} = \dfrac{6}{15}$

    N = _____

20. $\dfrac{6}{15} = \dfrac{10}{N}$

    N = _____

21. $\dfrac{3}{5} = \dfrac{N}{15}$

    N = _____

 There are 20 cars in the parking lot. If 2 out of 5 cars are two-door models, how many two-door cars are in the lot?

_____

Practice with Proportion

Sometimes the cost of a certain quantity of items at a supermarket is given. You may want to buy a different number of items. You can use proportions to find the price of the number of items that you need.

Examples: You can buy three grapefruit for $1.00.

How much will one grapefruit cost?

$$\frac{1 \text{ grapefruit}}{N} = \frac{3 \text{ grapefruit}}{\$1.00}$$

$1.00 \times 1 = 3 \times N$

$$\frac{1.00}{3} = N$$

$.33333333 = N$

One grapefruit costs 34 cents.

How much will five grapefruit cost?

$$\frac{3 \text{ grapefruit}}{\$1.00} = \frac{5 \text{ grapefruit}}{N}$$

$3 \times N = \$1.00 \times 5$

$$\frac{5.00}{3} = N$$

$1.6666666 = N$

Five grapefruit cost $1.67.

When you work with money, remember to round your answers to the next highest cent, as grocery stores do.

 Use a proportion to find the cost of the items described.

1. soup
   3 cans for $1.89

   2 cans for _____

   Hint: $\frac{3 \text{ cans}}{1.89} = \frac{2 \text{ cans}}{N}$

2. frozen pizza
   2 pizzas for $6.75

   1 pizza for _____

   Hint: $\frac{2 \text{ pizzas}}{6.75} = \frac{1 \text{ pizza}}{N}$

3. sandwich rolls
   6 rolls for $1.49

   18 rolls cost _____

4. potatoes
   5 pounds for $3.45

   3 pounds cost _____

5. paper towels
   3 rolls for $3.59

   4 rolls cost _____

6. oranges
   10 for $2.99

   5 cost _____

Solving Proportions

A Write a proportion to find the cost of the items.

1. fruit cocktail
   4 cans for $4.96

   6 cans cost _____

2. broccoli
   2 packages for $2.56

   3 packages cost _____

3. soap
   4 bars for $3.56

   7 bars cost _____

4. peppers
   4 for $2.00

   7 peppers cost _____

5. crackers
   2 boxes for $4.48

   1 box costs _____

6. sodas
   6 bottles for $2.99

   4 bottles cost _____

7. shortening
   2 cans for $5.39

   3 cans cost _____

8. sour cream
   2 cartons for $2.38

   1 carton costs _____

B Proportions can be used to solve a variety of other word problems. Be careful to write both ratios in the same order.

9. Three pounds of hamburger will feed twelve persons. How much hamburger will be needed to feed feed eight persons?

   $$\frac{3 \text{ pounds}}{12 \text{ persons}} =$$

10. A car can travel 320 miles on eight gallons of gas. How far can it travel on one gallon of gas?

    $$\frac{320 \text{ miles}}{8 \text{ gallons}} =$$

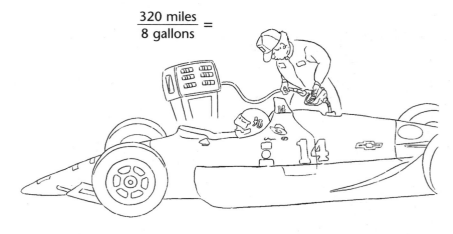

Word Problems with Proportion

Lesson 9

 Use a proportion to solve each problem.

1. Carmen can drive 240 miles in 5 hours. How far can she drive in 3 hours?

   _____

2. You make a snack by mixing 2 parts raisins to 3 parts peanuts. How many pounds of peanuts should you mix with one pound of raisins?

   _____

3. Sunrise red paint is made by mixing 4 parts of red paint with one part of yellow paint. How much yellow would you mix with 3 pints of red paint?

   _____

4. One U.S. dollar equals .73 in a foreign currency. How much would $10.85 U.S. currency be in the foreign currency?

   _____

5. The scale on a map is 1 cm to 20 km. How far apart are two towns that are 6.8 cm apart on the map?

   _____

6. Ron's car goes 28 miles on one gallon of gas. How far can he drive on 8 gallons of gas?

   _____

7. At Brubaker College there are 5 women for every 4 men. If there are 485 women, how many men are there?

   _____

8. Mix 3 liters of water with 9 lemons to make lemonade. How many lemons should you mix with 5 liters of water?

   _____

9. Oranges are selling at the rate of 12 oranges for $3.60. How much do 28 oranges cost?

   _____

10. Camp Whippoorwill employs 2 counselors for each 15 campers. How many counselors are needed for 120 campers?

    _____

Introducing Percents

Percents are based on 100 parts. If our work is 75% complete, then 75 parts out of 100 are finished. We can also think about percents in terms of a shape containing 100 squares.

This large block has a total of 100 smaller blocks; 17 of these blocks are shaded.

We can say this in three different ways:

$\frac{17 \text{ shaded}}{100 \text{ total}}$ or 17 per 100 shaded

OR

17 percent (17%)

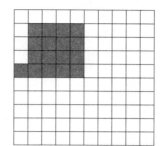

Percents can sometimes be written as fractions. Fractions and percents can both mean a portion of the whole.

■ Write the fraction and the percent that represent the area shaded.

1. 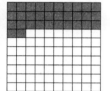 ____ and ____%

2. 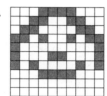 ____ and ____%

3. 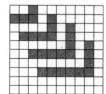 ____ and ____%

4. 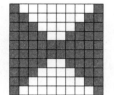 ____ and ____%

5. 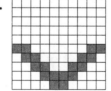 ____ and ____%

6. 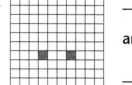 ____ and ____%

7. 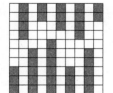 ____ and ____%

8. 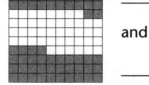 ____ and ____%

9. 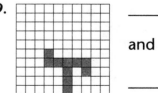 ____ and ____%

Solving for Percents

We can think of percents as ratios. Ratios compare two numbers. Percents compare a part to a whole. The "whole" is always 100 when you are working with percents.

Example: Jason got 87 words right on a test that contained 100 words. What was his test score?

$\frac{87 \text{ right}}{100 \text{ total}}$ equals 87% because the denominator is 100.

Sometimes the whole is not given as 100. You have to change your ratio to parts per 100. You can do this by using proportions.

Example: Three out of four doctors recommend this medication.

What percent of the doctors recommend this medication?

$\frac{3 \text{ recom.}}{4 \text{ total}} = \frac{N \text{ recom.}}{100}$ "N" will be the percent because the denominator is 100.

4 x N = 3 x 100
4 x N = 300
N = 300 ÷ 4   or   N = 75
The correct answer is 75%.

 Write a percent to tell what part of the whole is described. Write any remainders as a fraction.

1. Four out of five people like Muncho Chips.
____%

2. The Fighting Lizards have won 3 of their 10 games so far.
____%

3. Three-fifths of those interviewed are going to vote for Paco.
____%

4. Seven-eighths of the town came to the fair.
____%

5. One-third off of all prices.
____%

6. Mary got 4 hits for 7 times at bat.
____%

7. Lu Wen can make 9 out of 10 shots from the foul line.
____%

8. Two-thirds of the neighborhood attended the meeting.
____%

9. Four members of the class of 24 were absent.
____%

 Use a calculator to solve this problem. It rained 7 days during the past 3 weeks. What percent of the days were rainy? _____

Decimals and Percents

You can write a decimal as a percent by moving the decimal point two places to the right.

Examples: .48 = 48%   .236 = 23.6%   2.4 = 240%

A Rename each decimal as a percent.

1. .72 = _____%   2. .39 = _____%   3. .07 = _____%   4. .54 = _____%

5. .26 = _____%   6. 1.12 = _____%   7. 1.4 = _____%   8. .81 = _____%

9. 1.65 = _____%   10. .43 = _____%   11. .02 = _____%   12. .746 = _____%

13. .026 = _____%   14. 1.1 = _____%   15. .01 = _____%   16. .103 = _____%

17. 1.24 = _____%   18. .33 = _____%   19. 7 = _____%   20. .034 = _____%

21. 2.04 = _____%   22. 0.23 = _____%   23. 1.2 = _____%   24. 2.2 = _____%

25. 0.03 = _____%   26. 0.111 = _____%   27. 11.2 = _____%   28. 0.25 = _____%

You can also write a percent as a decimal. To write a percent as a decimal, move the decimal point two places to the left.

Examples: 42% = .42   6% = .06   132% = 1.32   20% = .20 or .2
                (final zeros may be dropped)

B Rename each percent as a decimal.

29. 46% = _____   30. 60% = _____   31. 8% = _____   32. 56% = _____

33. 80% = _____   34. 254% = _____   35. 1% = _____   36. 183% = _____

37. 92% = _____   38. 1.2% = _____   39. 120% = _____   40. 17.5% = _____

41. 2% = _____   42. .021% = _____   43. 2.2% = _____   44. 352% = _____

45. 5% = _____   46. 3.11% = _____   47. .11% = _____   48. 96% = _____

49. 1.3% = _____   50. 12.3% = _____   51. 41% = _____   52. 1.023% = _____

53. 2.22% = _____   54. 0.03% = _____   55. 0.01% = _____   56. 0.019% = _____

Renaming Percents

Percents are also like fractions. Both percents and fractions are parts of a whole. You can change a percent to a fraction. All you have to do is multiply the percent times $\frac{1}{100}$. Always simplify your answers if possible.

% means "times one-hundredth" or " x $\frac{1}{100}$."

Example: Change each percent to a common fraction. Write your answers in lowest terms.

$64\% = \frac{16}{25}$ $\qquad$ $5\% = \frac{1}{20}$ $\qquad$ $8\frac{1}{3}\% = \frac{1}{12}$

$64\% \times \frac{1}{100} = \frac{64}{100} = \frac{16}{25}$ $\qquad$ $5 \times \frac{1}{100} = \frac{5}{100} = \frac{1}{20}$ $\qquad$ $8\frac{1}{3} \times \frac{1}{100} = \frac{25}{3} \times \frac{1}{100} = \frac{25}{300} = \frac{1}{12}$

A Rename each percent as a common fraction. Write your answers in lowest terms.

1. 28% = _____
2. 8% = _____
3. 11% = _____
4. 44% = _____

5. 105% = _____
6. 85% = _____
7. 72% = _____
8. $2\frac{1}{2}\%$ = _____

9. $33\frac{1}{3}\%$ = _____
10. 14% = _____
11. 7% = _____
12. $18\frac{1}{3}\%$ = _____

13. 120% = _____
14. 48% = _____
15. $12\frac{1}{2}\%$ = _____
16. 2% = _____

B Fractions, decimals, and percents can all be used to express the same quantity. Fill in the missing values on these two charts.

	Fraction	= Decimal	= Percent
17.	$\frac{3}{4}$		
18.		.36	
19.			16%
20.	$\frac{2}{3}$		
21.			8%
22.	$\frac{13}{20}$		
23.		.4	
24.		.148	
25.	$\frac{7}{40}$		

	Fraction	= Decimal	= Percent
26.			50%
27.		2.6	
28.	$\frac{5}{6}$		
29.			48%
30.		.05	
31.			55%
32.		.26	
33.	$\frac{3}{5}$		
34.			35%

Huang and Julia were shopping for fruit drinks. Huang wanted to buy a 46-ounce can that was labeled "14% real fruit juice." Julia thought a can of the same size that advertised "$\frac{1}{6}$ real fruit juice" was a better buy. Which product had more real fruit juice?

_____

Percent of a Number

We can use mathematics to find out what a certain percent of a number is. This percentage is found by multiplying the base times the rate.

Example: What is 20% of 60?

RATE x BASE = PERCENTAGE

Step 1: Identify the rate. The rate is the number followed by the % sign. Change the rate to a decimal. 20% = .2

Step 2: Identify the base. The base is also called the whole. 60

Step 3: Multiply the rate times the base. .2 x 60 = 12.0

Step 4: Your answer is the percentage. 20% of 60 = 12

Example: What is 16% of 42?

Step 1: 16% = .16

Step 2: .16 x 42

Step 3: 16% of 42 = 6.72

$$\begin{array}{r} 42 \\ \times\, .16 \\ \hline 252 \\ 42 \\ \hline 6.72 \end{array}$$

A Find the percentages. Change the rate to a decimal.

1. 30% of 42 is _____.
2. 6% of 20 is _____.
3. 72% of 45 is _____.
4. 36% of 40 is _____.
5. _____ is 20% of 35.
6. .4% of 15 is _____.
7. _____ is 29% of 80.
8. _____ is 5% of 48.
9. _____ is 75% of 64.

Another way to find a percentage is to change the rate (or percent) to a fraction before you multiply.

Examples: What is 6% of 25?   What is 3% of 20?

Step 1: $6\% = \dfrac{6}{100}$ $3\% = \dfrac{3}{100}$

Step 2: $\dfrac{6}{\underset{4}{1\cancel{00}}} \times \overset{1}{\cancel{25}} = \dfrac{6}{4}$ $\dfrac{3}{\underset{5}{1\cancel{00}}} \times \overset{1}{\cancel{20}} = \dfrac{3}{5}$

$\dfrac{6}{4} = 1\dfrac{2}{4} = 1\dfrac{1}{2}$

Step 3: 6% of 25 is $1\dfrac{1}{2}$. $\dfrac{3}{5}$ is 3% of 20.

B Find the percentages. Change the rate to a fraction.

10. 36% of 75 is _____.
11. 8% of 95 is _____.
12. 80% of 62 is _____.
13. 6% of 50 is _____.
14. 20% of 35 is _____.
15. _____ is 40% of 28.
16. _____ is 5% of 60.
17. 85% of 200 is _____.
18. _____ is 25% of 8.

Discounts

Sometimes salespeople will deduct an amount from the selling price of an item. This discount is the amount that you can save. Multiply the list price times the rate of discount to find the discount.

LIST PRICE x RATE OF DISCOUNT = DISCOUNT

Example: The list price of a sweater is $45.65. The rate of discount is 9 percent. How much is the discount?

Step 1: Change the rate to a decimal or fraction. $9\% = .09$ $9\% = \frac{9}{100}$

Step 2: Multiply rate x base. $.09 \times \$45.65$ $\frac{9}{100} \times \$45.65 = \frac{410.85}{100}$

$$\begin{array}{r} \$45.65 \\ \times\ .09 \\ \hline 4.1085 \end{array}$$

Step 3: The discount is $4.11. $4.1085 = 4.11$ $4.1085 = 4.11$

When working with money, always round your answer to the next highest cent.

 Find the discount on these various items.

1. Pair of pants
   List Price $24.95
   Rate of Discount 20%

   DISCOUNT = _____

2. Television set
   List Price $245.00
   Rate of Discount 15%

   DISCOUNT = _____

3. Lawn mower
   List Price $145.90
   Rate of Discount 12.5%

   DISCOUNT = _____

4. Shirt
   List Price $24.35
   Rate of Discount 25%

   DISCOUNT = _____

5. Radio
   List Price $24.00
   Rate of Discount 8%

   DISCOUNT = _____

6. Belt
   List Price $18.49
   Rate of Discount 2.5%

   DISCOUNT = _____

7. Wallet
   List Price $40.80
   Rate of Discount 23.3%

   DISCOUNT = _____

8. Stereo system
   List Price $1,229
   Rate of Discount 16%

   DISCOUNT = _____

9. Sunglasses
   List Price $15.00
   Rate of Discount 15%

   DISCOUNT = _____

10. Leather jacket
    List Price $185.00
    Rate of Discount 30%

    DISCOUNT = _____

11. Bicycle
    List Price $85.50
    Rate of Discount 35%

    DISCOUNT = _____

12. Bedsheets
    List Price $23.80
    Rate of Discount 40%

    DISCOUNT = _____

Solving for the Sale Price

The sale price is the new amount that an item sells for. It is found by subtracting the discount from the list price.

Example:

Shoes	$ 49.50	list price	$49.50	list price
List Price $49.50	x .20	discount rate	− 9.90	discount
Rate of Discount 20%	$9.9000	discount	$39.60	sale price

 Find the amount of the discount and the sale price for these items.

1. Wheelbarrow
   List Price $125.50
   Rate of Discount 24%

   DISCOUNT = _____

   SALE PRICE = _____

2. Socks
   List Price $1.89
   Rate of Discount 8%

   DISCOUNT = _____

   SALE PRICE = _____

3. Canoe
   List Price $208.00
   Rate of Discount 16%

   DISCOUNT = _____

   SALE PRICE = _____

4. Cologne
   List Price $32.50
   Rate of Discount 20%

   DISCOUNT = _____

   SALE PRICE = _____

5. Tie
   List Price $17.60
   Rate of Discount 30%

   DISCOUNT = _____

   SALE PRICE = _____

6. Drill press
   List Price $389.00
   Rate of Discount 18%

   DISCOUNT = _____

   SALE PRICE = _____

7. Wristwatch
   List Price $37.95
   Rate of Discount 16%

   DISCOUNT = _____

   SALE PRICE = _____

8. Scarf
   List Price $18.60
   Rate of Discount 25%

   DISCOUNT = _____

   SALE PRICE = _____

9. Backpack
   List Price $29.89
   Rate of Discount 35%

   DISCOUNT = _____

   SALE PRICE = _____

 Jeff bought a sofa for $600, 2 lamps for $80 each, a chair for $350, and a table for $210. The store advertised 20% off purchases totaling $1,000 or more. How much did Jeff pay for his new furniture?

_____

Adding Time

Elapsed time means time that has gone by. To find out what the time will be after a certain time has elapsed, you add the present time to the elapsed time. Add hours to hours and minutes to minutes. If the minutes in your answer are 60 or more, then subtract 60 from the minutes and add 1 to the hours. If the hours in your answer are more than 12, then subtract 12.

Example: 6 hours 42 minutes

```
  2:15    present
+ 6:42    elapsed
  8:57    new time
```

Add to find the time that will be on each clock after the given amount of time has passed.

1.   3 hr. 10 min.

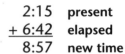

_____

2.   4 hr. 28 min.

1:42

_____

3.   6 hr. 13 min.

_____

4.   6 hr. 8 min.

1:43

_____

5.   2 hr. 56 min.

_____

6.   5 hr. 37 min.

_____

7.   3 hr. 17 min.

_____

8.   7 hr. 21 min.

_____

9.   3 hr. 14 min.

2:42

_____

Alpesh left his home at 2:15 to visit a friend in the next state. He drove for 5 hours and 23 minutes. At what time did Alpesh reach his friend's house?   _____

Subtracting Time

To find out how much time has elapsed, you subtract the time shown on one clock from the time shown on a second clock. In subtraction, you sometimes have to rename. One hour equals 60 minutes. Therefore, you can rename 1 hour to 60 minutes.

Example: Subtract the time on Clock A from the time on Clock B to find the elapsed time.

CLOCK A	CLOCK B	CLOCK A	CLOCK B

Clock B: 5:23 = 4:83 (23 + 60 = 83)   Clock B: 1:28 = 13:28 (add 12 hours)
Clock A: − 2:35 = 2:35   Clock A: − 11:15 = 11:15
              2:48 elapsed time   2:13 elapsed time

■ Subtract to find the amount of time that has elapsed from the time shown on Clock A to the time shown on clock B.

	CLOCK A	CLOCK B		CLOCK A	CLOCK B
1.		 _____	2.		_____
3.		_____	4.		 _____
5.		 _____	6.		 _____
7.		_____	8.		_____
9.		_____	10.		_____

Measuring Inches

Before you can measure a line using a ruler, you need to know what the little marks on the ruler stand for. Look at the first inch on the ruler.

One inch:

Divided into two parts:

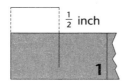

Divided into eight parts:

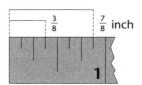

Divided into four parts:

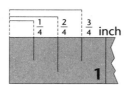

Divided into sixteen parts:

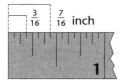

Write the length of each line segment shown below.

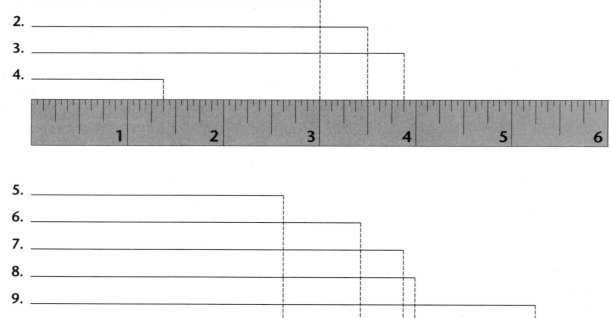

1. _____

2. _____

3. _____

4. _____

5. _____

6. _____

7. _____

8. _____

9. _____

10. _____

11. _____

Changing Linear Measurements

Multiply or divide when changing to other units of length. When you change from a large unit of length to a smaller unit, you multiply by the conversion factor. When you change from a small unit of length to a larger unit, you divide by the conversion factor.

Unit of length		Conversion factor
1 foot	=	12 inches
1 yard	=	36 inches
1 yard	=	3 feet
1 mile	=	5,280 feet
1 mile	=	1,760 yards

Examples:

4 yards = ? inches
Large to Small —
Multiply by the conversion factor.
1 yard = 36 inches
36 x 4 = 144
4 yards = 144 inches

51 feet = ? yards
Small to Large —
Divide by the conversion factor.
3 feet = 1 yard
51 ÷ 3 = 17
51 feet = 17 yards

 Fill in the missing numbers.

1. 72 inches = _____ feet

2. 3 miles = _____ yards

3. 7 feet = _____ inches

4. 1 mile = _____ inches

5. 147 feet = _____ yards

6. 4 miles = _____ feet

7. 48 inches = _____ feet

8. 10,560 feet = _____ miles

9. 288 inches = _____ yards

10. 23 feet = _____ inches

11. 5 feet = _____ inches

12. 9 yards = _____ feet

13. 14 feet = _____ inches

14. 156 inches = _____ feet

15. 17,600 yards = _____ miles

16. 18 feet = _____ inches

 Mario is a cross-country runner. He trains 5 days a week. Each day he runs 10,560 yards. How many miles does Mario run each week?

_____

Adding and Subtracting Linear Measurements

When you add or subtract measurements, you can only combine units that are the same. You can add feet to feet and inches to inches, but not inches to feet. Sometimes you have to change one unit to another.

12 inches = 1 foot   **3 feet = 1 yard**

Example: Find the answers.

2 yards	1 foot	8 inches
+ 1 yard	1 foot	7 inches
3 yards	2 feet	15 inches

or

3 yards 3 feet 3 inches
(or 4 yards 3 inches)

	1	20
2 yards	2̶ feet	8̶ inches
− 1 yard	1 foot	9 inches
1 yard	0 feet	11 inches

or

1 yard 11 inches

Find the answers to these problems. Do not introduce new or larger units into the answer. If the answer is 8 feet 7 inches, then do not convert feet to yards unless yards were given in the problem.

1.

2 feet	8 inches
+ 1 foot	2 inches

2.

6 yards	2 feet	3 inches
− 2 yards	1 foot	10 inches

3.

3 yards	1 foot	8 inches
+ 2 yards	1 foot	7 inches

4.

7 feet	3 inches
+ 9 feet	8 inches

5.

4 yards	2 feet	5 inches
− 1 yard	2 feet	7 inches

6.

4 yards	8 inches
− 2 yards	11 inches

7.

8 yards		10 inches
+ 3 yards	2 feet	7 inches

8.

2 yards		9 inches
− 1 yard	2 feet	6 inches

Area is a two-dimensional measure of how much surface is in a region. Area is measured in square units such as square inches (sq. in.) or square feet (sq. ft.). You can find the area of a rectangle by multiplying its length by its width.

Example: Find the area of this rectangle.
A = length x width
A = 3 units x 2 units
A = 6 square units

The area is 6 sq. units.

■ Find the area of each rectangle. Remember to include the correct units in each answer.

1.   2 in.
4 in.

Area = _____

2. $3\frac{1}{4}$ in.
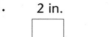 $\frac{3}{4}$ in.

Area = _____

3.   4.2 in.
1.6 in.

Area = _____

4. $1\frac{1}{2}$ ft.
$2\frac{1}{3}$ ft.

Area = _____

5. $\frac{3}{8}$ in.
4 in.

Area = _____

6.   3 ft.
$5\frac{1}{2}$ ft.

Area = _____

7.   .12 ft.
4.3 ft.

Area = _____

8.   .6 in.
2.1 in.

Area = _____

9. $2\frac{2}{3}$ ft.
$\frac{3}{4}$ ft.

Area = _____

10. $1\frac{1}{2}$ in.
6 in.

Area = _____

11.   1.6 in.
4.2 in.

Area = _____

12.   1.2 in.
1.2 in.

Area = _____

13. $1\frac{2}{3}$ in.
$\frac{3}{5}$ in.

Area = _____

14. $\frac{2}{3}$ in.
$1\frac{1}{8}$ in.

Area = _____

15. $1\frac{1}{3}$ in.
$4\frac{1}{2}$ in.

Area = _____

 Michelle is planning to purchase new carpeting for her family room. The room measures 14 feet x 18 feet. How much carpeting should Michelle buy?
a. 252 feet   **b.** 32 square feet
c. 64 square feet   **d.** 252 square feet

_____

Volume is the measurement of three-dimensional space, such as the space inside a room or a ball. Volume is measured in cubic units such as cubic inches (cu. in.) or cubic feet (cu. ft.). The volume of a shape is the measure of how much it holds. You can find the volume of a rectangular prism by multiplying its length, width, and height.

Example: Find the volume of a rectangular prism with a length of 3 inches, a width of 2 inches, and a height of 2 inches.

Volume = length x width x height
$V = l \times w \times h$
$V = 3 \times 2 \times 2$
$V = 12$ cu. in.
The volume is 3 x 2 x 2, or 12 cu. in.

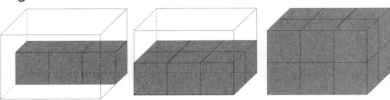

Find the volume of each rectangular prism.

1.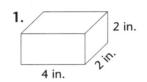
2 in., 2 in., 4 in.

_____

2.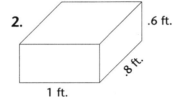
.6 ft., .8 ft., 1 ft.

_____

3.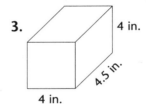
4 in., 4.5 in., 4 in.

_____

4.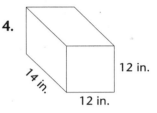
12 in., 12 in., 14 in.

_____

5.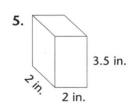
3.5 in., 2 in., 2 in.

_____

6.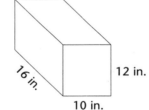
16 in., 12 in., 10 in.

_____

7.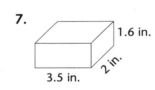
1.6 in., 2 in., 3.5 in.

_____

8.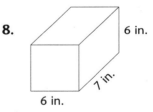
6 in., 7 in., 6 in.

_____

9.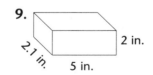
2 in., 2.1 in., 5 in.

_____

10.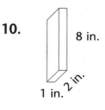
8 in., 1 in., 2 in.

_____

11.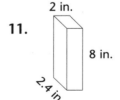
2 in., 8 in., 2.4 in.

_____

12.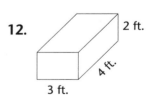
2 ft., 4 ft., 3 ft.

_____

13.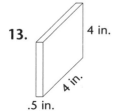
4 in., 4 in., .5 in.

_____

14.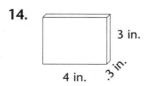
3 in., 4 in., .3 in.

_____

15.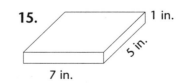
1 in., 5 in., 7 in.

_____

16.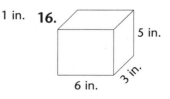
5 in., 6 in., .3 in.

_____

Measuring with Metrics

Lesson 8

The measurements we have used so far are part of a system called *English,* or *customary,* measurement. There is also another system that we can use. It is called the *metric* system. Sometimes it is easier to work with the metric system because it is based on powers of 10.

Look at this drawing of a metric ruler. Each numbered spaces is one centimeter. Each little space is one millimeter. You can count the little spaces to see that 10 millimeters are in 1 centimeter.

Example: Measure the length of this pencil to the nearest centimeter and to the nearest millimeter.

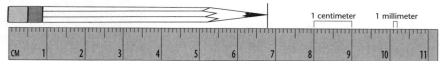

The length to the nearest centimeter is 7 centimeters, or 7 cm.
The length to the nearest millimeter is 68 millimeters, or 68 mm.

Use a centimeter ruler. Measure the length of each pencil to the nearest centimeter and the nearest millimeter.

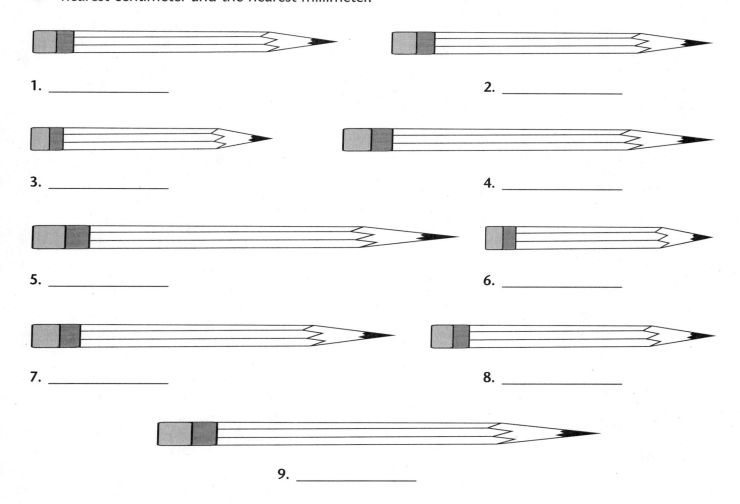

1. _____

2. _____

3. _____

4. _____

5. _____

6. _____

7. _____

8. _____

9. _____

Changing Metric Measurements

When you convert metric measurements from one unit to the other, you multiply or divide by 10, 100, 1,000 and so on. Since these are all powers of ten, you can think of moving the decimal point to the right or left instead of actually multiplying or dividing.

Use this diagram to help you change from one unit to another.

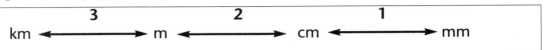

Larger unit to smaller unit

Multiply by moving the decimal point to the right.

Example:

To change meters to centimeters, move the decimal point 2 places to the right.

5.2 m = 5.20 = 520 cm

Smaller unit to larger unit

Divide by moving the decimal point to the left.

Example:

To change millimeters to meters, move the decimal point 1 + 2 = 3 places to the left.

63 mm = 063. = .063 m

A Fill in the missing numbers.

1. 48 mm = _____ cm
2. 25 m = _____ cm
3. 6 km = _____ m
4. 25 cm = _____ mm
5. 5.2 cm = _____ mm
6. 4200 mm = _____ km
7. 7 m = _____ cm
8. 4.5 m = _____ cm
9. 420 mm = _____ m
10. .042 km = _____ cm
11. 3.07 m = _____ mm
12. 45.3 cm = _____ mm
13. .007 m = _____ mm
14. 25,000 cm = _____ km
15. 4600 m = _____ km
16. .042 cm = _____ mm
17. 24 mm = _____ cm
18. .048 m = _____ mm
19. 650 mm = _____ m
20. 720 mm = _____ cm
21. .6 km = _____ m

B You can add only like units. If the units are not the same, you have to convert them before adding.

22. 16 cm + 23 cm = _____ cm
23. 12 cm + 43 mm + 36 cm = _____ cm
24. 6 cm + 42 mm = _____ mm
25. 4.7 cm + 28 mm + 52 cm = _____ mm
26. 28 mm + 7.3 cm = _____ cm
27. 9.3 cm + 6 m + 4 mm = _____ cm
28. 72 cm + 4 m = _____ cm
29. 5 mm + 8 cm + 3 m = _____ cm

George rode his bicycle 2,000 meters to school and 2.9 kilometers to the library. Gina rode 4,800 meters to the recreation center. Who rode the shorter distance?

_____

Area with Metrics

Area (or the space enclosed within lines) can also be measured using the metric system. Area is measured in square units. These include square millimeters (mm^2), square centimeters (cm^2), and square meters (m^2). This is what two of those measures actually look like.

▫ 1 mm^2

 1 cm^2

To find the area, use the formula you already know.

AREA = LENGTH x WIDTH

Example:

AREA = LENGTH x WIDTH

A = 5 cm x 2 cm

A = 10 cm^2

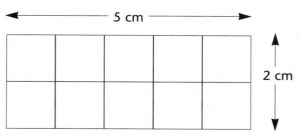

■ Find the area of each rectangle. Name each unit correctly.

1. 5.3 cm
1.2 cm

_____

2. 1.2 cm
5.6 cm

_____

3. 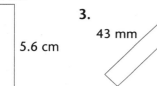 8 mm
43 mm

_____

4. .8 cm
4 cm

_____

5. 23 mm
12 mm

_____

6. 16 mm
4 mm

_____

7. 23 mm

_____

8. 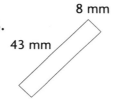 .8 cm
8 mm
1.6 cm

_____

9. 1.2 m
3.4 m

_____

10. 5.1 cm
5.1 cm

_____

11. 2.3 cm
2.3 cm

_____

12. 4.2 cm
8 cm

_____

13. 21 mm
18 mm

_____

14. .8 cm
.6 cm

_____

15. 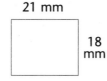 12.3 mm
.8 mm

_____

Converting Units of Liquid Capacity

Capacity means the amount of liquid a container can hold. When you change from a large unit of capacity to a smaller unit, you multiply by the conversion factor. When changing from a small unit of capacity to a larger unit, you would divide by the conversion factor. This table shows the conversion factors for units of liquid capacity.

Unit of capacity		Conversion factor
1 pint (pt.)	=	16 ounces (oz.)
1 pint (pt.)	=	2 cups (c.)
1 quart (qt.)	=	2 pints (pt.)
1 gallon (gal.)	=	4 quarts (qt.)

Examples:

5 quarts = _____ pints

Large to Small — **Multiply** by the conversion factor

1 quart = 2 pints

5 x 2 = 10

5 quarts = 10 pints

12 quarts = _____ gallons

Small to Large — **Divide** by the conversion factor

1 gallon = 4 quarts

12 ÷ 4 = 3

12 quarts = 3 gallons

 Fill in the blanks.

1. 6 pt. = _____ oz.

2. 12 qt. = _____ pt.

3. 8 pt. = _____ qt.

4. 20 pt. = _____ c.

5. 96 oz. = _____ pt.

6. 10 gal. = _____ oz.

7. 216 oz. = _____ pt.

8. 14 qt. = _____ c.

9. 1 qt. 1 pt. = _____ pt.

10. 18 pt. = _____ gal.

11. $5\frac{1}{2}$ gal. = _____ qt.

12. 2 pt. 3 oz. = _____ oz.

13. 3 c. = _____ oz.

14. 33 pt. = _____ qt.

15. 4 gal. 2 qt. = _____ qt.

16. 23 gal. = _____ qt.

17. 25 qt. = _____ pt.

18. 10 pt.= _____ oz.

 Jackie filled her fish tank with 13 quarts of water. Two months later the fish tank contained 3 gallons of water. How many cups of water had evaporated?

_____

Circumference of a Circle

The distance around a circle is called the *circumference.* When you find the circumference of a circle, you are finding out how far it is around the circle. The *diameter* of a circle is the distance across the circle at its widest point. One-half the diamater is called the *radius.* If you divide the circumference by the diameter, you will always get a number that is a little greater than 3. This ratio is known by the Greek letter π, which is pronounced like *pie.* The value of π is approximately 3.14.

Radius = *r*   **Diameter = *D***   **Circumference = 2 π r**

Example: Use the formula $C = 2 \pi r$ to find the circumference of these circles.
Remember: $\pi = 3.14$.

4 in.

$C = 2 \pi r$
$C = 2 \times 3.14 \times 4$
$C = 25.12$ inches

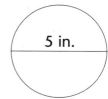

5 in.

Since $d = 5$ in., $r = 2.5$
$C = 2 \pi r$
$C = 2 \times 3.14 \times 2.5$
$C = 15.7$ inches

 Use the formula $C = 2 \pi r$ to find the circumference of these circles.
Remember: $\pi = 3.14$.

1. $r = 5$ inches

C = _____

2. $r = 8$ cm

C = _____

3. $D = 6$ cm

C = _____

4. $D = 9$ mm

C = _____

5. $D = 7$ inches

C = _____

6. $D = 2$ m

C = _____

7. $r = 13$ mm

C = _____

8. $D = 20$ mm

C = _____

9.

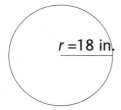

$r = 18$ in.

C = _____

10.

D = 22 m

C = _____

11.

10 cm

C = _____

12.

24 in.

C = _____

13.

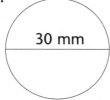

30 mm

C = _____

14.

16 cm

C = _____

15.

3.5 in.

C = _____

16.

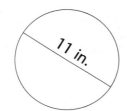

11 in.

C = _____

Area of a Circle

The *area* of a circle is the measure of how much surface is inside the circle. Area is given in square units. Find the area of a circle by multiplying π times the radius times the radius, or area = π r^2. π can be expressed as either 3.14 or as $\frac{22}{7}$.

Examples: Find the area for each circle. Use 3.14 for π.

 6 in.

Area = π r^2
Area = 3.14 x 6 x 6
Area = 113.04 sq. in.

 2.4 in.

$A = π r^2$
A = 3.14 x 2.4 x 2.4
A = 18.0864 sq. in.

A Find the areas of these circles. Use π = 3.14.

1.  2 in.

2. 1 cm

3. 3 mm

4. 5 cm

5.  .1 cm

_____ _____ _____ _____ _____

6. .4 cm

7. 20 mm

8.  4.2 in.

9.  15 cm

10. 9 in.

_____ _____ _____ _____ _____

Examples: Find the area for each circle. Use $\frac{22}{7}$ for π.

 7 cm

$A = π r^2$

$A = \frac{22}{7} \times \frac{7}{1} \times \frac{7}{1}$

$A = 22 \times 7$

$A = 154 \text{ cm}^2$

 $1\frac{1}{2}$ in.

$A = π r^2$

$A = \frac{22}{7} \times \frac{3}{2} \times \frac{3}{2}$

$A = \frac{198}{28}$ or $7\frac{1}{14}$ sq. in.

B Use π = $\frac{22}{7}$ to find the area of these circles.

11.  1 m

12. 7 mm

13. $3\frac{1}{2}$ in.

14. 3 mm

15. 21 cm

_____ _____ _____ _____ _____

16. $\frac{1}{2}$ m

17. $2\frac{1}{3}$ in.

18. 4 cm

19. 10 mm

20. $\frac{7}{11}$ in.

_____ _____ _____ _____ _____

Metric Volume

Volume is measured in cubic units such as cubic millimeters (mm³), and cubic meters (m³).

cubic millimeter: cubic centimeter:

Example: Find the volume of a rectangular prism having a length of 3 cm, a width of 2 cm, and a height of 2 cm.

Volume = length x width x height
V = 3 cm x 2 cm x 2 cm
V = 3 x 2 x 2
V = 12 cm³

One row of 3 cm³
3

Two rows of 3 cm³
3 x 2

Two layers
of 6 cm³
3 x 2 x 2

Find the volume of each rectangular prism.

1.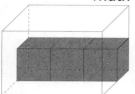
9 cm
16 cm   7 cm

_____

2.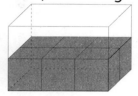
4 cm
8 cm   16 cm

_____

3.
5 cm
22 cm   20 cm

_____

4.
10 cm
15 cm   30 cm

_____

5.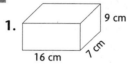
8 mm   12 mm
35 mm

_____

6.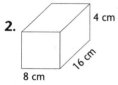
3 mm   20 mm
15 mm

_____

7.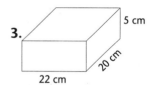
20 cm   11 cm
30 cm

_____

8.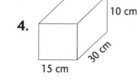
20 cm
20 cm   8 cm

_____

9.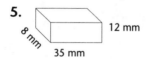
24 mm
8 mm   20 mm

_____

10.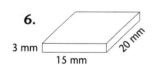
35 mm   12 mm
10 mm

_____

11.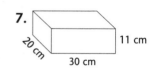
4 cm
18 cm   8 cm

_____

12.
9 cm
10 cm   18 cm

_____

13.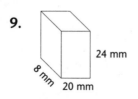
12 cm
14 cm   6 cm

_____

14.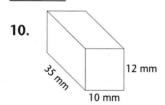
12 mm
2 mm   20 mm

_____

15.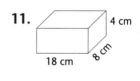
2 mm   10 mm
12 mm

_____

16.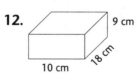
18 cm
20 cm   16 cm

_____

Proficiency Test 4

■ Circle the correct answer

1. Which ratio is equal to $\frac{6}{8}$?
   a. $\frac{10}{20}$
   b. $\frac{2}{3}$
   c. $\frac{15}{20}$
   d. $\frac{12}{20}$

2. If 3 pounds of bananas sell for $1.00, how much do 5 pounds cost?
   a. $1.66
   b. $3.00
   c. $1.67
   d. $2.00

3. 12.6 renamed as a percent is
   a. 1260%
   b. 12.6%
   c. 120.6%
   d. 1.26%

4. 24% renamed as a fraction is
   a. $\frac{6}{25}$
   b. $\frac{1}{4}$
   c. $\frac{1}{5}$
   d. $\frac{5}{25}$

5. 60% of 160 is
   a. 60
   b. 96
   c. 9.6
   d. 16

6.   4 yards 2 feet 8 inches
    + 1yard   1 foot 2 inches

   a. 5 yards 10 inches
   b. 3 yards 1 foot 6 inches
   c. 5 yards 3 feet 12 inches
   d. 6 yards 10 inches

7. 65% renamed as a fraction is
   a. $\frac{2}{3}$
   b. $\frac{1}{2}$
   c. $\frac{35}{65}$
   d. $\frac{13}{20}$

8. A sweater that has a list price of $44 is on sale for $39.60. What is the rate of discount?
   a. 10%
   b. 20%
   c. 5%
   d. 30%

9. How many inches are in 9 feet?
   a. 84 inches
   b. 112 inches
   c. 108 inches
   d. 27 inches

10. 12 yards – 1 yard 2 feet 2 inches
   a. 12 yards 2 feet 2 inches
   b. 12 yards 1 foot 10 inches
   c. 11 yards 2 feet 2 inches
   d. 10 yards 10 inches

11. What is the area?
   4 feet wide by 32 feet long
   a. 72 feet
   b. 128 sq. feet
   c. 64 sq. feet
   d. 36 feet

12. 41 m + 16 m =
   a. 57 m
   b. 57 mm
   c. 5.7 cm
   d. .57 km

13. How many ounces are there in 11 pints?
   a. 176 ounces
   b. 44 ounces
   c. 88 ounces
   d. 22 ounces

14. What is the circumference?
   a. 62.8 cm
   b. 40 cm
   c. 125.6 cm
   d. 1256 cm

15. What is 110% of 230?
   a. 23
   b. 200
   c. 250
   d. 253

16. What is the volume?
   a. 9 mm^3
   b. 24 cm^3
   c. 13 mm^3
   d. 12 mm

17. What is the area of a circle with a radius of 5 inches?
   a. 15.7 inches
   b. 78.5 inches
   c. 25 inches
   d. 31.40 inches

18. 4.6 m + 23 cm =
   a. 27.6 cm
   b. 2.76 cm
   c. 483 cm
   d. 483 m

19. If a car travels 420 miles on 20 gallons of gas, how far can it travel on 1 gallon?
   a. 21
   b. 20
   c. 42
   d. 25

20. A car that costs $13,400 is selling at 8% discount. What is the discount?
   a. $107.20
   b. $1,072.00
   c. $1,004.00
   d. $1,172.00

End-of-Book Test

Circle the correct answer.

1. $4.78 + $1.56 + $3 =
   a. $6.37
   b. $9.34
   c. $8.24
   d. $8.34

2. 5,403 − 1,278
   a. 3,125
   b. 4,275
   c. 4,225
   d. 4,125

3. 1,359
    875
    4,637
    + 2,482

   a. 9,253
   b. 9,353
   c. 10,353
   d. 10,253

4. What is the area?
   a. 77.7 cm²
   b. 117 cm²
   c. 77 cm²
   d. 71.7 cm²

   7 cm
   11 cm

5. The numeral for "six million, one hundred twelve" is
   a. 6,100,012
   b. 6,112,000
   c. 6,112
   d. 6,000,112

6. 1564 ÷ 34 =
   a. 52
   b. 47
   c. 46
   d. 56

7. 6 ÷ .02 =
   a. 300
   b. 30
   c. 3
   d. .3

8. 246 x 65 =
   a. 2,706
   b. 15,990
   c. 16,090
   d. 16,990

9. Rename $\frac{5}{8}$ as a decimal.
   a. .58
   b. .62
   c. .625
   d. .16

10. $\frac{3}{5} \times 3\frac{3}{4} =$
    a. $\frac{9}{20}$
    b. $2\frac{1}{4}$
    c. 3
    d. $9\frac{7}{5}$

11. $2\frac{2}{3} + 4\frac{5}{6} =$
    a. $6\frac{7}{9}$
    b. $7\frac{1}{2}$
    c. $6\frac{1}{2}$
    d. $7\frac{1}{6}$

12. $\frac{3}{8} + \frac{5}{6} =$
    a. $1\frac{1}{14}$
    b. $\frac{7}{24}$
    c. $1\frac{5}{16}$
    d. $1\frac{5}{24}$

13. $\frac{4}{7} \times \frac{5}{6} =$
    a. $\frac{10}{21}$
    b. $\frac{24}{35}$
    c. $1\frac{11}{24}$
    d. $\frac{3}{14}$

14. $\frac{7}{8} - \frac{1}{4} =$
    a. $1\frac{1}{2}$
    b. $\frac{3}{7}$
    c. $\frac{5}{8}$
    d. $\frac{3}{4}$

15. Which fraction is larger than $\frac{5}{6}$?
    a. $\frac{5}{7}$
    b. $\frac{7}{9}$
    c. $\frac{11}{13}$
    d. $\frac{3}{4}$

16. $3\frac{1}{3} - \frac{5}{6} =$
    a. $2\frac{1}{2}$
    b. $3\frac{1}{2}$
    c. $3\frac{4}{3}$
    d. $3\frac{3}{4}$

17. What is the area?
    a. 36 cm²
    b. 36 cm
    c. 26 cm²
    d. 26 cm

    4 cm
    9 cm

18. 3.24 + 1.3 + 15 =
    a. 4.69
    b. 19.54
    c. 3.42
    d. 20.64

19. $\frac{5}{6} \div \frac{2}{3} =$
    a. $\frac{4}{5}$
    b. $1\frac{1}{2}$
    c. $\frac{5}{9}$
    d. $1\frac{1}{4}$

20. $1\frac{1}{3} \div 1\frac{2}{3} =$
    a. $\frac{1}{2}$
    b. $1\frac{1}{4}$
    c. $\frac{4}{5}$
    d. $1\frac{1}{3}$

21. $\frac{4}{5}$ is what percent?
    a. 4%
    b. 5%
    c. 20%
    d. 80%

22. 23 − .06 =
   a. 23.94
   b. 23.06
   c. 22.94
   d. 22.84

23. .23 x .006 =
   a. .138
   b. .0138
   c. .00138
   d. .000138

24. The numeral for "seven thousandths" is
   a. .007
   b. .7000
   c. .0007
   d. 7000

25. How long is the line segment?

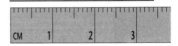

   a. 3.5 mm
   b. 3.4 mm
   c. 3.5 cm
   d. 3.4 cm

26. $24.38
   x   35

   a. $852.30
   b. $853.30
   c. $743.59
   d. $195.04

27. What is 20% of 65?
   a. 15
   b. 12
   c. 13
   d. 14

28. $8 − $.34 =
   a. $7.34
   b. $8.34
   c. $7.76
   d. $7.66

29. Lemons sell for 6 for $1.98. How much will 4 cost?
   a. $1.32
   b. $1.64
   c. $1.31
   d. $1.50

30. What percent of 30 is 12?
   a. 40%
   b. 25%
   c. 42%
   d. 32%

31. You spend $14.32. What change should you get from $20.00?
   a. $6.68
   b. $6.78
   c. $5.78
   d. $5.68

32. What is the average of 39, 43, 28, 36, and 29?
   a. 30
   b. 35
   c. 40
   d. 175

33. Which decimal is larger than .52?
   a. .149
   b. .4306
   c. .398
   d. .6

34. What is the volume?
   a. 11 cm^3
   b. 11 cm
   c. 40 cm^3
   d. 40 cm

5 cm   4 cm   2 cm

35. What is the best way to find how many $1.75 comic books you can buy with $12?
   a. add
   b. subtract
   c. multiply
   d. divide

36. There are 70 students in the class; 40% are boys. How many are girls?
   a. 28
   b. 60
   c. 57
   d. 42

37. How long is the segment?

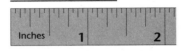

   a. $1\frac{3}{8}$"
   b. $1\frac{1}{2}$"
   c. $1\frac{7}{8}$"
   d. $1\frac{1}{4}$"

38. What is 34,723 rounded to the nearest thousand?
   a. 34,000
   b. 35,000
   c. 30,000
   d. 34,700

39. What is .2437 rounded to the nearest hundredth?
   a. .244
   b. .243
   c. .25
   d. .24

40. How many quarts are there in 7 gallons?
   a. 28
   b. 14
   c. 56
   d. 70